COWBRIDGE AND LLANBLETHIAN
AN HISTORICAL MEDLEY

COWBRIDGE AND LLANBLETHIAN

An Historical Medley

Edited by
Brian James

COWBRIDGE HISTORY SOCIETY
2016

Published by
Cowbridge History Society,
Stallcourt Mews
Llanblethian,
Cowbridge CF71 7JU

Printed by
Keith Brown and Sons Ltd
55 Eastgate, Cowbridge

www.brownsprinters.co.uk

ISBN 0 9537029-8-7

CONTENTS

PREFACE

This is the first book to be published by the Cowbridge History Society, but it continues the series of eight volumes previously published by the Cowbridge Record Society which merged with the Cowbridge and District Local History Society in 2013.

Newsletters have been an important feature of these societies since 1977, for many years edited by Jeff Alden. Much valuable information has been included in the many articles in the newsletters - indeed, some were on subjects that have never been written about elsewhere. Our Chairman suggested that a selection of these articles, which might otherwise become forgotten, would form the basis for a book. This is the book; but also included are talks given to the societies and one or two other contributions which add to our knowledge of the history of Cowbridge and Llanblethian. Some of the articles have been revised in the light of more recent research.

The Society is grateful to Deborah Fisher, R. J. Buswell, Betty Whyatt, Brian James, Nicole Burnett, Don Gerrard and Nigel Williams for their ready agreement to allow their articles to be reprinted in this book. We owe a special word of appreciation to the families of the late Jeff Alden and the late Luke Millar for permission to publish their articles. Regrettably, it has not been possible to identify the copyright owner of the late Selwyn Davies's reminiscences; we hope that we may be forgiven for this omission.

We also acknowledge permission to publish copyright material in the possession of the Warwickshire County Record Office, the Glamorgan-Gwent Archaeological Trust and the Royal Commission on the Ancient and Historical Monuments of Wales.

Many of the illustrations in this volume, from the collection at the Local History Study Room in Old Hall, have been digitised by Betty Alden and John Sherwood; we are grateful for their invaluable help.

The Society's Committee hopes that readers will find the varied content of this book - truly a 'medley' - interesting and readable.

B. J.

1236.—Anne, Queen of Richard III.

Anne Neville at her coronation.
From a Victorian print, based on the fifteenth-century Rous Roll.

ANNE NEVILLE, PRINCESS OF WALES, QUEEN OF ENGLAND, AND LORD OF GLAMORGAN

By Deborah Fisher

Some readers may be wondering what connection there could be between a medieval queen of England and a town in South Wales. Others will be aware of the links between Anne Neville and the churches of Cowbridge. I first gave a talk about her at a meeting of the Cowbridge Record Society (forerunner of Cowbridge History Society), therefore the focus was on illustrating how records contribute to our understanding of her life and her connection with us. Her story demonstrates that, not only can records tell us a lot about the past, but the very absence of records can affect our view of past events.

Anne Neville died at the age of twenty-eight. In her time she held the titles of Princess of Wales, Duchess of Gloucester and Queen of England, in that order. She had an eventful life by most people's standards, yet we know very little about her, as is the case with many medieval queens. Some would say this is only to be expected, as a queen consort had no share in governing the kingdom. Yet we know that some queens had a very strong influence, and we will see that this was also the case with Anne.

The only picture of Anne that is near contemporary appears in the Rous Roll, a genealogical record of her family. One of the most useful sources of historical knowledge for the past 150 years has been the photograph, but in mid-fifteenth-century England, not only did they not have photography, they had no proper portraiture. The portraits of monarchs at the National Portrait Gallery only really begin with Edward IV, and the painting of him is one of the first that bears any suggestion of being true to life. Women would have to wait a few years longer to be considered important enough for their appearance to be recorded with any care.

Anne was born at Warwick Castle on 11th June 1456. We know this much, which is more than we can say of many other royal women of the time. She was the second child of Richard Neville, Earl of Warwick, whom we know as 'the Kingmaker'. Some people are under the impression that Warwick the Kingmaker changed sides several times during the Wars of the Roses; in fact he only did so once. Neville had come by the title of Earl of Warwick through his wife, Anne Beauchamp, who was the daughter of the previous earl, Richard Beauchamp. That might be regarded as good luck, but it was Neville's *bad* luck that, like his father-in-law, he had no sons to succeed him, only two daughters, Isabel and Anne.

Neville was a wealthy, powerful man. The earldom of Warwick brought him vast estates (including the lordship of Glamorgan) to add to those of the earldom of Salisbury, which he held in his own right. He owned several castles; a favourite was Middleham in the north of England, where his children spent a lot of their time. When the two girls were born, Henry VI was on the throne. Although Henry had been king from the age of nine months, the country had been run by regents until he came of age. He then married Margaret of Anjou, who would gain the nickname 'the Tigress of France', for her role in the Wars of the Roses, and they had only one child - Edward, Prince of Wales, usually known as Edward of Westminster to differentiate him from all the other Edwards that were around at the time.

One of those other Edwards was the Earl of March, the eldest son of the Duke of York. York, who happened to be an uncle of Richard Neville's wife, had a strong claim to the throne and, until the birth of the Prince of Wales, he had hoped to be Henry VI's successor. By the time Edward of Westminster was born, King Henry was already in the grip of mental illness, and there were rumours that the child was not really his. The Yorkists took up arms against the king, and thus began the Wars of the Roses. At the Battle of Northampton in 1460, the Yorkists were victorious; they took the king prisoner and forced him to agree to disinherit his own son and make the Duke of York his heir.

Queen Margaret's response was to raise an army of her own, which defeated York later in the same year. The Duke was killed, which made his son, Edward, Earl of March, the Yorkist claimant to the throne. This is where the kingmaking abilities of the Earl of Warwick came into play. Richard Neville was thirty-two years old at the time, and he went into exile along with the young Earl of March, who was only eighteen. One of the Duke of York's sons was killed along with his father at the Battle of Wakefield, but there were two younger sons, George and Richard. They came under the protection of the Earl of Warwick and went into his household.

So at Middleham Castle we have four children growing up: George, Duke of Clarence, aged eleven, his brother Richard, aged eight, and

Warwick's two daughters, Isabel Neville, aged nine, and Anne, aged four. We might like to guess at the outcome, but in truth we have little idea what happened during those years. Children's activities were not carefully recorded. There were no school photographs, no concerts to be video-recorded, and most of the time we cannot even be sure who was where. We can only surmise that the four children became close friends.

In the meantime, the Earl of March, despite his youth, showed himself to be a military genius, and with Warwick's help he became King Edward IV of England. Henry VI was deposed and put into confinement, whilst Queen Margaret and her son escaped to France. The Earl of Warwick was well in with the new young king. It was a few years before King Edward started to want to be free of the earl's influence. One of the first signs of this was when Edward, knowing that Warwick was negotiating for him to marry a foreign princess, got secretly married to an English widow, Elizabeth Woodville, whose family had been *Lancastrian* supporters in the recent war! Things got worse, as the Woodville family took over prominent positions at court and Warwick was sidelined.

In 1469, the king's brother, George, Duke of Clarence, married Isabel Neville, his childhood companion. Like Warwick, he was growing tired of the king's new in-laws. So he agreed when Warwick suggested that they should all go to France and find Margaret of Anjou. This was the one and only time that Warwick turned coat. He went to Margaret and offered to help restore her husband's throne. Henry VI was in Yorkist hands, but Margaret's main concern was to get her son's inheritance back. As proof of good faith she insisted that Warwick go back to England and get the throne back before she and her son followed. In return, she agreed to his proposal that her son, Edward of Westminster, aged seventeen, should marry Warwick's daughter, Anne, who was now about fourteen.

This is where the lack of records, combined with our lack of understanding of the period, again makes it difficult for us to know what was going on. We are not sure when the marriage took place, but after December 1470 Anne was married to the Prince of Wales, making her Princess of Wales. Or was she? It is unclear whether the ceremony that took place was a wedding or just a betrothal. Even if the records were more complete, we could not necessarily be sure of the answer, because a promise to marry someone was regarded as legally binding. We are not sure whether it was a marriage, or just an arrangement that Margaret of Anjou could get out of later if Warwick let her down. We don't know whether the marriage, if it was one, was ever consummated.

There is no record of Anne being called Princess of Wales, so we do not know whether she ever used the title. It would hardly be surprising if she did not, because the title of Prince of Wales had only been held by four princes before Edward of Westminster - it was still not automatic - and the title of Princess of Wales had only been held by one woman before Anne. However, let us assume that Anne was Princess of Wales when the news reached France that her father, the Earl of Warwick, had defeated King Edward IV in battle and had restored King Henry VI to the throne. Edward IV had been forced to flee the country, and it was safe for Margaret of Anjou, together with her son and daughter-in-law, to return.

Not everything was going according to plan. Warwick's other son-in-law had deserted him. It had suddenly dawned on the rather unintelligent Clarence that, if the Lancastrians got the throne back, he was never actually going to be king himself whereas, if he went over to his brother's side, he would at least have some standing. Warwick, despite his experience, was no great diplomat. By accepting French help, he had turned the Burgundians against him, and it was to Burgundy, where his sister was duchess, that Edward IV went, returning before Margaret of Anjou arrived. The Lancastrian royal party reached England's shores to be greeted with the news that the Earl of Warwick, on whom they had relied, was dead, and Henry VI was back in prison - where he soon 'died'.

We can only imagine what this must have been like for Anne, but we do not know her reaction. In fact, we do not know exactly where she was in the period after she returned to England. We know that Margaret tried to join forces with the one man who might have changed the course of history, clever old Jasper Tudor, but they were prevented from meeting up in time by the obstacle of the River Severn.

At the Battle of Tewkesbury, on 4 May 1471, Edward of Westminster was killed - the only Prince of Wales ever to be killed in battle. Or was he? Actually, some accounts say that he was killed *after* the battle, when many of his army took refuge inside Tewkesbury Abbey and were slaughtered by the Yorkists. It is said that Anne and her mother-in-law took refuge in a religious house. This may have been Malvern Priory, which has a window donated by Anne and her second husband, but there is no proof of her having been there, only oral tradition and some generally unreliable written sources. If she was - and it is certainly quite plausible - it goes some way to explaining her later interest in religious foundations.

The next time Anne surfaces in the records is not until 1472, and by then she has remarried, and her new husband is none other than her childhood companion, Richard, Duke of Gloucester. We know they were married in that year, but we do not know exactly when their son - yet another Edward - was born, although we do know that he was born at Middleham Castle, hence he is referred to as Edward of Middleham.

What was Anne doing in the fourteen months between the end of her first marriage and the beginning of her second one? The popular story may have a grain of truth in it, but is not supported by any official records. Anne was brought to London in the train of her victorious brother-in-law, Edward IV. There is no reason to think she was ill-treated or even treated as a prisoner. Although she was Warwick's daughter and the widow of Henry VI's son and heir, she was also a long-standing friend of the family, and her sister was married to the king's brother. Perhaps Anne had never been happy as the wife of the Prince of Wales - just imagine having Margaret of Anjou as a mother-in-law. Even if she had loved her first husband, she was probably relieved at seeing those familiar faces, the family of the Duke of York.

Moreover, Anne had potential financial value. She is said to have run away from her brother-in-law, Clarence, who was now responsible for his widowed sister-in-law. It is certain that Clarence and his youngest brother, Richard, Duke of Gloucester, were not on good terms. They were jockeying for position. Clarence had been disloyal to his brother, the king, but, like the Prodigal Son, he had returned to the fold. It must have seemed hard to Richard, who had stood by Edward through thick and thin, that Clarence should receive a share of the rewards. But there was more to it than that.

Because Warwick was dead, his inheritance, and the estates of his wife Anne Beauchamp (who was still alive at this time), passed jointly to his daughters and their husbands. Isabel Neville was married to Clarence and they had children, therefore Clarence stood to gain if anything happened to Isabel's sister, Anne. However, he had everything to lose if Anne decided to marry his brother, Richard, who was already his greatest rival. Whether or not Richard and Anne had been close when they were children, it would seem a reasonable idea for them to marry, and we can understand why Clarence might have kidnapped her, which is another version of the story. Whether he did this or whether she was in hiding from him, she is said to have been discovered working as a kitchen-maid in London, and rescued - by Richard, Duke of Gloucester.

This supposed act of heroism has become part of the great myth surrounding Richard III about which I would like to say something, but not too much. After Henry VII took the throne, he did his best to make Richard out to be a villain. Tudor supporters were prepared to invent stories about Richard in order to win Henry's favour. The recent discovery of Richard's bones throws little light on his personality, but does demonstrate one thing: not all Tudor 'propaganda' was mere propaganda. The severe spinal deformity, from which we now know that he suffered, would in those days have been considered evidence of an evil character, which helped Henry discredit him. One more thing Henry did, which would backfire on the Tudors a long time afterwards, was to destroy a lot of the records relating to Richard's reign. Because those records no longer exist, there are many things we cannot be sure about.

In the last fifty years or so, it has become fashionable to take the view that, because the Tudors made up stories about Richard III, he must therefore have been innocent of all crimes of which he was accused. Many people fail to understand that the concept of recording history accurately is a relatively modern one. Medieval historians were not concerned with truth; the word 'historia', in Latin, means 'a story'. From the few facts that are available, we know that Richard III had by far the best motive and opportunity for murdering his two nephews, the Princes in the Tower. It is a matter of historical record that the rumours of his having killed them were circulating as early as January 1484, when Henry Tudor was still a refugee in France. Most damning of all, despite knowing about these rumours and publicly denying them, Richard made no attempt to disprove them by allowing the boys to be seen in public. They were never seen alive after the autumn of 1483.

Many have difficulty understanding how a king who is recorded as having been very popular in parts of the country, particularly the north, a man who endowed places of worship and educational establishments, could have done something as repellent as to kill two children who were related to him - the sons of a brother to whom he was very close. 'Ricardians' believe that Richard was a good man, and therefore could never have done anything bad. Yet it is a matter of record that Richard had already had the two princes, his brother's children, declared illegitimate, in order to take the throne from them. Richard foresaw that his nephew, Edward V, would be easily influenced by the Woodville family, and that the Woodvilles would resent Richard's position as Lord Protector and try to get rid of him. He got in first and made sure of his own safety and that of his family. Once the boys were in captivity, though, he had a problem: his enemies might have got hold of them and made them into figureheads and started another civil war. So they had to be removed. Of course Richard did not go into the Tower of London and strangle them with his own hands, but there was no shortage of people who would have been prepared to do it for him; he probably didn't need to ask.

Whatever happened to the two princes, we tend to assume that Richard's wife, Anne, didn't know much about it. For more than ten years, from the time of their marriage up to the sudden death of King Edward IV in 1483, they had lived quietly, as Duke and Duchess of Gloucester, in the north of England, mainly at Middleham Castle, the very place where they spent their childhood together. If Edward IV had lived a little longer, they might well have stayed there.

Edward's sudden death threw the country into turmoil, and pushed Anne Neville into the limelight. Because she left no stamp of her personality on things, we make the assumption, perhaps wrongly, that she was quiet, self-effacing, perhaps shy, easily pushed around and taken advantage of. We assume that she was happy with her husband and that she loved her family. Her sister, Isabel, had died and Isabel's husband, the Duke of Clarence, had been executed for treason. So Anne was responsible for the welfare of her sister's children as well as her own.

Founding churches and colleges was all part of the business of being wealthy and powerful. Anne Neville is supposed to have enlarged Llanblethian church. In 1721, it was recorded in Llanblethian parish register that Anne built the tower of the church, and also 'the south part of Cowbridge church and St John's Tower in Cardiff'. The same entry also says that her husband built 'the north gate of Cardiff Town', but also mentions that he became King of England 'by usurpation'.

Anne is supposed to have contributed towards the building or restoration of Holy Cross Church, and we know that Richard signed a charter relating to the appointment of a chaplain for Holy Cross. Some say that the name 'Llanquian' (as in the 'Llanquian aisle' of the church), is derived from the word 'queen'. I doubt that. Does this mean that either Richard or Anne ever came here? I don't think so. I have not come across any evidence that Anne Neville, either as Princess of Wales or as Queen of England, ever set foot in Wales.

Amongst other things, Anne had inherited from her father the lordship of Glamorgan, but it was Richard who took the title. Perhaps that in itself is enough to explain why they took an interest in the churches of Glamorgan. They took an interest in many other places. They founded or restored churches at Barnard Castle and Sheriff Hutton in the north of England, and they were generous benefactors of York Minster. They went to Cambridge, where Queens' College, originally founded by Margaret of Anjou, was re-endowed in Anne's name. In return, they could be assured of having prayers said for them in these places. But why did they need prayers? Was Richard simply a devout man who really cared about the Church, or was he appeasing his conscience? Some Ricardians pleaded for Richard to be buried according to Catholic rites in recognition of the fact that England was still a Catholic country during his lifetime. One outstanding tenet of Catholic belief is that the forgiveness of sins can be obtained by confession and repentance. Pardons could be bought and sold in the Middle Ages, and endowing a church would be enough to save your soul even if you *had* murdered your nephews.

However they came by their position as king and queen, Anne and Richard did not have long to enjoy it. Anne was probably already dying. She is thought to have had tuberculosis. She had given birth to only one child, her son Edward, who was invested as Prince of Wales in September 1483. He died only a few months later. The Croyland chronicle says that 'you might have seen his father and mother in a state almost bordering on madness by reason of their sudden grief'. Reading that is the only time I have ever felt sorry for Richard III.

Edward of Middleham had been heir to the throne, and he was replaced in that role by another Edward, his first cousin. This boy, Edward, Earl of Warwick, was the son of George of Clarence and Isabel Neville, so he was Anne's nephew as well as Richard's. It is interesting to note, however, that almost as soon as Anne died, Richard named a new heir, an adult relation, John de la Pole, Earl of Lincoln. He had presumably named Edward to please Anne, or maybe she had talked him into it, but once the threat of a Tudor invasion became real, he knew it would be unwise to have a child as his heir.

Anne survived her son by only eleven months, and no doubt his death contributed to her illness. She was young enough to have another child, but the fact that she only had one suggests a basic weakness in her constitution; her sister Isabel was equally delicate, and had died seven years earlier. It began to be said, quite openly, that Richard was planning to get rid of his wife and was intending to marry his niece, Elizabeth of York, in her place. Here is another example of how records can mislead the modern mind if we don't read them in context. Although the idea of marrying one's niece gives us a feeling of revulsion, it would have been considered quite acceptable as long as the Pope was prepared to give a dispensation. We do not know whether he would have, but we know that Richard made no move to marry Elizabeth after Anne's death.

Anne's death was expected, but did she die of natural causes, or had Richard been poisoning her over a long period, as the Tudors hinted? If we compare her with her sister, who was dead at twenty-five, we see that the family constitution was not exactly strong. Ill health was probably the reason she conceived no further children. For Richard to have murdered her, he would have needed a motive, and there is no obvious one apart from the desire to marry again, which he made no serious attempt to do. He died not long after his wife, at the Battle of Bosworth Field, and a Welshman, Henry Tudor, became King of England. For many years, there was not even a memorial to Anne Neville in Westminster Abbey, but eventually one was erected by the efforts of the Richard III Society. So the Ricardians have done something useful after all.

FURTHER READING

Fisher, Deborah, *Princesses of Wales* (Cardiff, University of Wales Press, 2005).

Gristwood, Sarah, *Blood Sisters: the Women behind the Wars of the Roses* (Harper Press, 2013).

Kendall, Paul Murray, *Richard III* (New ed., Norton, 2002).

ARCHAEOLOGY AND THE WAITROSE SITE: A NOTE

By R. J. Buswell

As part of the application to the Vale of Glamorgan Council for planning permission to build the Waitrose store in Cowbridge (which opened in October 2012), an archaeological assessment of the site was required. This was undertaken by Headland Archaeology of Hereford. Their report is attached to the planning application which can be found on the Vale of Glamorgan website using application number 2011/00423. Part of this note is drawn from that report, with the permission of the authors.

As a planned Anglo-Norman walled town founded in the thirteenth century, it is not surprising that most of the early core of the town was within these walls (fig.1). The town had the now familiar long street, burgage plot layout. It was designed primarily as an economic venture by the lord of Glamorgan to attract English settlers into this newly conquered territory in the Vale of Glamorgan by providing burgesses with market privileges and other benefits. The town walls served three purposes: as a defence against possible attack from the conquered Welsh, as a symbol of the new power of the Anglo-Norman lords and, economically, as a means of controlling the rights of traders who had settled in the town - charges would be levied on anyone seeking to enter the town for trading purposes.

What do we know about these walls? First, they were not very substantial. They were probably about three metres high in most places, with four gates at the cardinal compass points, only one of which survives - the often restored south gate - the remainder having been demolished in the eighteenth century, the east and west gates to permit better passage of traffic on the main road through the town. Secondly, we know now that most of what survives of the wall is probably eighteenth-century reconstruction (Jones, 17). It is likely that since about the fifteenth century the walls were robbed of their very valuable building stone and used in the construction of buildings within the town. What has survived from the original walls is the footings and part of the bastion in the south-west corner in Old Hall gardens together, possibly, with parts of the west wall between the bastion and the former *Masons Arms* (the Market Place Restaurant) (Jones, 18).

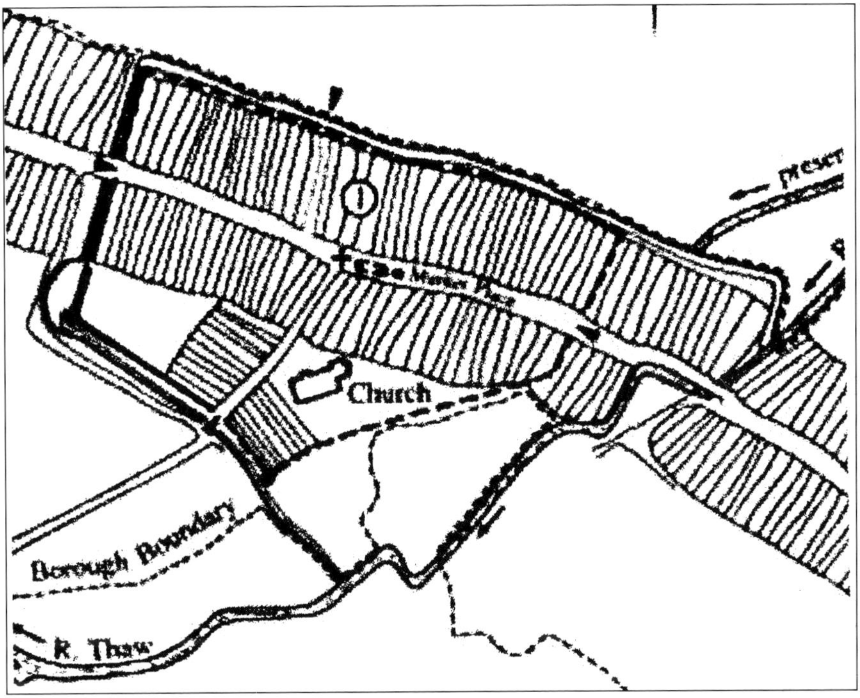

Fig. 1: The original walled town.
Royal Commission on the Ancient and Historical Monuments of Wales.

What has the archaeological report, made for the Waitrose planning application, added to our knowledge of the walls - and what else might it have found if further excavations had been carried out? It established the line of the medieval wall across the site, at a point about ten metres from the north-west corner of the front of the new store. Its position has been marked in the new surface of the car-park and roadway across the site. Excavation revealed four courses of rough stonework with lime mortar sitting on a rather narrow set of footings (figs. 2 and 3) (Headland, 4). The inside of the wall was probably robbed leaving largely rubble. The original wall was probably about two metres wide. Outside the wall ran the town ditch thought to have been two to six metres wide (Headland, 3). This may have had stagnant or slow moving water in it and was probably part of the defensive system of the town. Although it generally survived until the mid-eighteenth century, the ditch to the east seems to have lasted longer,

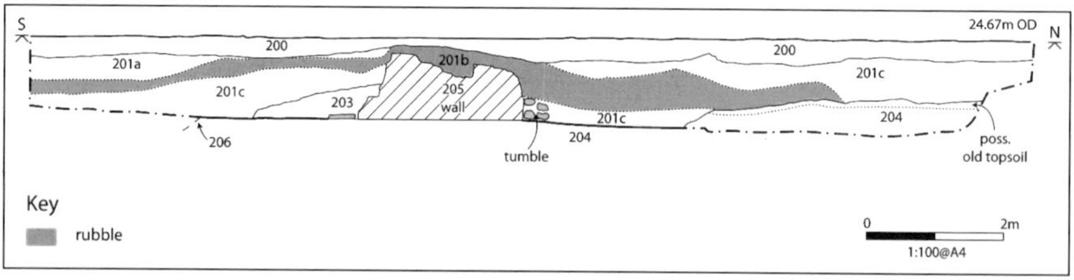

Fig. 2: Cross section of the remains of the east wall, Waitrose site. *Headland Archaeology.*

Fig. 3: The east wall excavated on the Waitrose site. *Headland Archaeology.*

until 1813, and 'in 1832 it was "cleansed" at the expense of the corporation' (Spurgeon, 185).

At this point of the town's topography, the wall would have crossed an alluvial plain of boulder clay and silt, part of the flood plain of the river Thaw. This marshy and probably often inundated area of land spread out widely on both sides of the river although on the east side the limestone country rock is soon encountered. (9 and 10 The Limes are built on it, a few metres above current river levels.) In the post-medieval era the area was probably left empty; there is no evidence of it ever having been built upon. However, during the late eighteenth and nineteenth centuries it was used as the town dump for ash. The coal and wood fires of the town's houses and workshops would have used large quantities of fuel and the waste (ashes) had to be disposed of. Where better than a marshy area liable to flooding - perhaps an early attempt at land reclamation.

The excavations revealed what is thought to have been a quite low town wall, as evidenced by the narrowness of the foundations, which suggests they could not have supported a wall as high as that from the south gate to the north-west bastion. It is suggested by the archaeologists that this could mean that to the east the town relied upon the river Thaw and its poorly drained flood plain for its defences. This also supports the idea that the walls of Cowbridge were not primarily there for defensive purposes but as a means of controlling ingress and egress.

On the map by C. J. Spurgeon in 2001 (fig. 4) the suggested line of the wall is shown crossing through the former garden centre. We now know its exact location accurately (see above). The line of the wall at that point has been projected in a more easterly direction via a series of stainless steel discs set in the asphalt. If Spurgeon's hypothesis is correct it should eventually meet part of the east wall which comes down the east side of the town hall to a point somewhere on the border of the Waitrose site/Birds Lane and the car park of 'Beauty Within'. Spurgeon suggested that at this junction there may well have been another bastion to accommodate the turn of the wall and to act as a defensive point (Spurgeon, 187).

The Headland archaeologists' report goes on to say:

> Based on the results of the evaluation and the map evidence it is considered that the potential for complex archaeological remains relating to the Roman or medieval occupations of Cowbridge to occur within the development area is low. The one exception to this is likely to be the point where the site access road is located on the medieval street frontage, and also along the line of the earlier Roman road, where the ribbon development could be expected to occur. Any ground works in this area are likely to encounter deposits relating to either or both these periods. It was not possible to evaluate the access lane due to continual usage and the presence of major services. (Headland, 9).

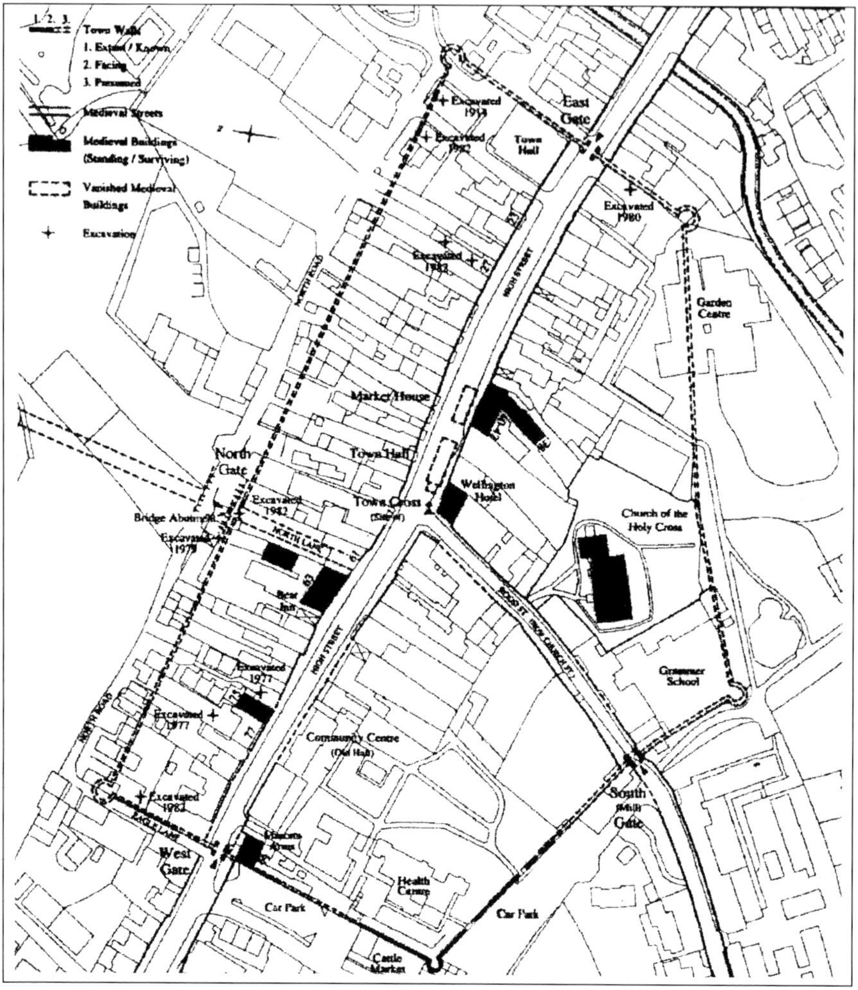

Fig. 4: Possible line of town wall. Note position suggested for corner bastion near the entrance to the Waitrose site. *Royal Commission on Ancient and Historical Monuments of Wales.*

In December 2010 Neil Maylan of the Glamorgan-Gwent Archaeological Trust wrote the following memorandum to Dale Evans of Alder King Partners, the consulting planners employed by Birds soon after the Headland Archaeology report was finished:

> Thank you for sending me a copy of your proposed plan. After Headland had done their evaluation I found that an article had been published in *Studia Celtica* that included a projected layout of the walls of Cowbridge that shows that a tower may be located in the development area (see attached report and especially the plan on page 180). The good news is that you have no major structures planned for this site which would appear to be located to the northeast of the row of small shops close to the entrance. This may be an interesting feature to look for during the development giving a potential opportunity for display in order to enhance the development.

In the first part of the last sentence appears to be a lost opportunity to discover what may have been a significant element in Cowbridge's medieval townscape. Perhaps funds can be found to erect a plaque marking the spot.

By 1269 the walled town's burgage plots must have been mostly occupied and the town would then have spread east and west of the walls along the Portway enabling more plots to have been laid out. Medieval Cowbridge then declined until its revival in the sixteenth century and again in the eighteenth century.

REFERENCES

Jones, Peter, 'Cowbridge town walls past and present', in *Echoes of Old Cowbridge* (Cowbridge Record Society, 2011), pp. 9-29.

Robinson, David M., *Cowbridge: the Archaeology and Topography of a Small Market Town* (Swansea, Glamorgan-Gwent Archaeological Trust, 1980).

Spurgeon, C. J., 'The medieval town defences of Glamorgan', *Studia Celtica,* XXXV (2001), pp. 177-87.

ACKNOWLEDGEMENTS

Thanks to Headland Archaeology (UK) Ltd, Neil Maylan, Jeffrey Bird, Vale of Glamorgan Planning Department and Alder King Consultants for permission to draw on various documents and to reproduce some of the illustrations.

BURGAGE RENTALS

By Jeff Alden

Among the most significant recent [2003] finds relating to the history of Cowbridge has been the discovery at the National Library of Wales, Aberystwyth, of the lists of burgage rents payable to the Marquess of Bute and his predecessors as lords of the borough of Cowbridge.

Cowbridge, as a medieval planted town, was also a planned town. The major element of this planning was the burgage plot: the long, narrow strip of land usually extending back from the main street to the boundaries of the borough. A house or workshop would be built on the street side (often end-on), with garden and outbuildings behind. The standard yearly rent for a single burgage in Cowbridge - as in most other towns in England and Wales - was one shilling. Robinson's book on the archaeology and topography of Cowbridge points out that in 1263 (nine years after the grant of the first charter by Richard de Clare) the town yielded fixed rents amounting to £2 19s. He then deduces that in 1263 the population of Cowbridge occupied about 59 burgage tenements. Using the same method of calculation he suggests that the number of burgages had risen to 135 in 1281 and 233 in 1295. Even by the end of the thirteenth century, however, the number of burgages did not necessarily represent the number of households, as some burgages had been subdivided and other plots amalgamated. But the figures must indicate that the population was increasing rapidly in those early years of the town's history.

The earliest of the 'Burgage Rentals' is for 1738. This certainly shows evidence both for subdivision and amalgamation, as there were many half-burgages and one (Old Hall) was rated at twelve and a half burgages. The total within the walls is 58¾ burgages, as far as I can work out, suggesting that the population in 1263 was solely within the walls, and that the town soon spread out beyond the physical limits of the walls into Westgate and Eastgate. Remarkably, the total number of burgages in 1738 seems to be 232½ (virtually the same as in 1295), which would have rendered £11 12s 6d to the lord (Viscount Windsor at that date), had it been possible to gather in all the rents due (which is unlikely to have been the case).

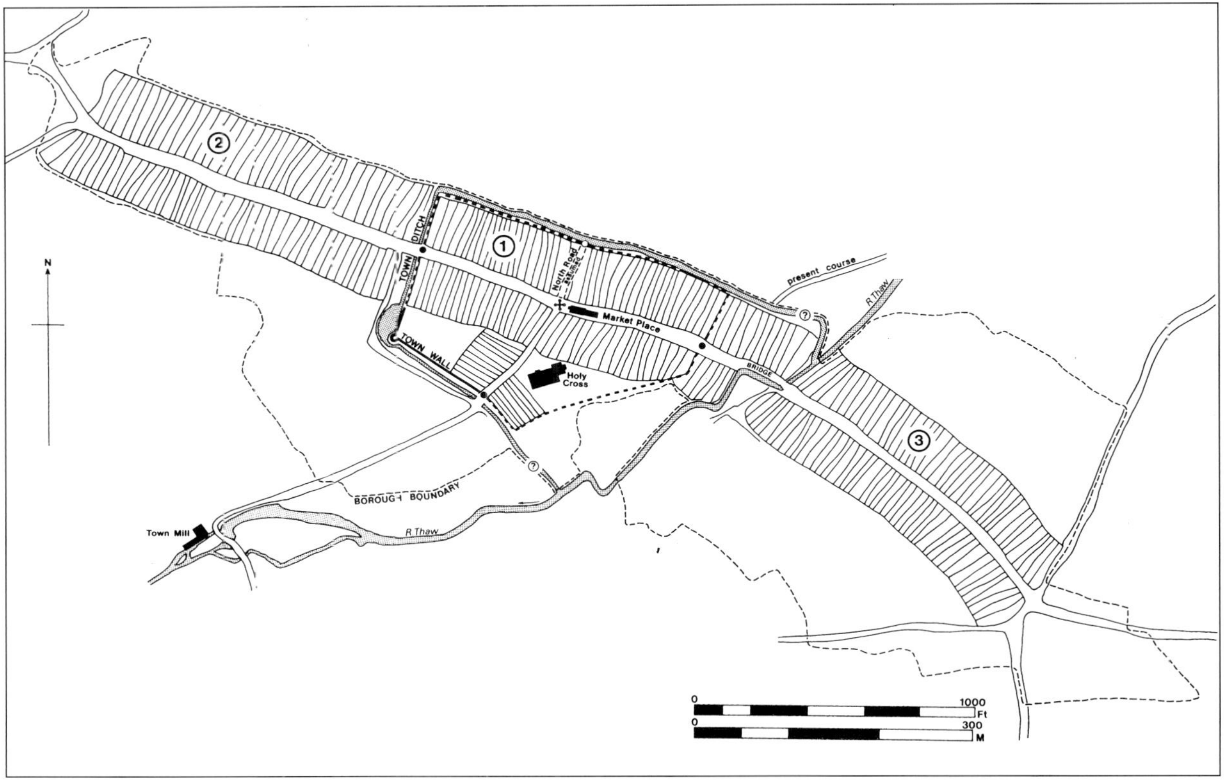

Conjectural reconstruction of burgage plots, with other features of medieval Cowbridge, after David M. Robinson
Glamorgan-Gwent Archaeological Trust.

What is of great importance to anyone attempting to repopulate the town is that the lists always start at the west end, work systematically eastwards along the south side of the High Street (with minor incursions into Church Street and the Limes) and then, on reaching the eastern limit of the borough, work westwards along the northern edge of the High Street. For each property in 1738 we have the name of the owner and the size of the plot (in terms of burgages). By 1744 we also have the name of the tenant, and this information is provided in all later rentals. There are some gaps in the records, but fortunately very little change in number or size of holdings is shown for the period 1738 to 1834 covered by these rentals. So the rentals have proved extraordinarily useful in working out who lived where.

The earliest date of a land tax assessment for Cowbridge is 1773, but using the burgage rentals we can now go back a further thirty-five years, with much more detailed records. There are problems, as different officials varied in working out who was a freeholder, a tenant, a lessee or an occupier. It is also clear that some of the rent collectors copied out older lists without making many, if any, amendments, even though some of the people named had died or moved away.

Despite the difficulties, for many properties we can follow ownership and tenancy clearly throughout the period. There are also great leaps forward to be made when links can be established with title deeds. A remarkable example is that there was only one plot in all Cowbridge rated at three-eighths of a burgage. So when a deed mentions a plot as being 'one quarter of a burgage and a half of one quarter' it is in all likelihood the same property. In this way the history of 79 High Street can be pushed back to 1603, when Matilda John alias Hughes, widow, and John Hughes (probably her son) conveyed this property to Robert Robinson, M.A., the Vicar of Llanblethian, and he subsequently conveyed it to William Morrice, tailor, and so on. (These seventeenth-century deeds are preserved in the Edmondes Collection in the Glamorgan Archives.)

Perhaps even more important is that knowledge of the ownership of specific properties in the burgage rentals has enabled us to correct the errors of an eighteenth-century lawyer's clerk (and also the errors of a much more recent editor). The deeds for an inn called the *Half Moon,* belonging to Pierce Cornish, have one entry stating that the house in question was 'on the west of Church Street'. For the account in *Cowbridge: Buildings and People* (p. 65) I used this location and so placed the *Half Moon* at 50 High

Street. The burgage rentals, however, make it quite clear that Pierce Cornish's property was what we now know as the *Duke of Wellington* - 48 High Street, on the east side of Church Street. Small corrections need to be made to the book!

SOURCES

The Cowbridge burgage rentals are in the National Library of Wales, Bute Estate Records R6/20-1.

The land tax assessments are among the Glamorgan county records and the Cowbridge borough records in the Glamorgan Archives.

Alden, Jeff (ed.), 'Cowbridge High Street. Sources and References', 2003. A copy of this unpublished document can be seen in the Local History Studies Room, Old Hall.

Robinson, David M., *Cowbridge: the Archaeology and Topography of a Small Market Town in the Vale of Glamorgan* (Swansea, Glamorgan-Gwent Archaeological Trust, 1980).

Spurgeon, C. J., 'The medieval town defences of Glamorgan', *Studia Celtica*, XXXV (2001), pp. 177-87.

THE STORY OF COWBRIDGE AND WATER: 760 YEARS OF STRUGGLE

By R. J. Buswell

Introduction

Cowbridge is a small but important historic town in the Vale of Glamorgan. It is a planned town planted by the Anglo-Normans in the thirteenth century when Richard de Clare, the Lord of Glamorgan, granted a charter to the town in 1254. The town was laid out along the old Roman road, with a series of regular burgage plots at right angles on either side of this road (fig.1, see p. 25). It is one of the few walled towns of Wales not dominated by a castle. In medieval times it was one of a small number of major urban centres in South Wales, with market and administrative functions. It did not receive its first supply of piped water until 1926.

Water was, and still is, a precious commodity which even in wet Wales has quite a high value even if supply may seem infinite. The town's connections with water go back to its very origins as it is located on the River Thaw (Ddawan in Welsh) where an early bridge traversed poorly drained land before crossing the river itself. In many ways water was to define Cowbridge: it is there in its English name, and in Welsh where Y Bont-faen means 'the stone bridge'.

Sources of water and their uses

Historically, until the technologies of capturing water for year-long supply and its distribution to every household, business and industry were introduced, water for consumption had strictly limited geographical boundaries partly determined by geology. It was essentially a locally produced and consumed commodity. Cowbridge is sited on Lias and Carboniferous Limestone, rock structures that are noted for their permeable characteristics. Only where the water-table reaches the surface is there accessible water. To the north and south of the town are low-lying, poorly drained and marshy areas; numerous springs decant water from the lower slopes of the surrounding hills. Surface water regularly disappears

Fig. 2: The old stone bridge over the River Thaw, c.1905. *Editor's Collection.*

down sink-holes, only to emerge later, lower downstream. Because the water-table is fairly near the surface after heavy rains it is not surprising the town has, historically, been subject to numerous floods.

Cowbridge, from the late thirteenth century, was a walled town with four gates, one at each of the principal compass points. Beyond the walls lay the Town Ditch, originally dug for defensive purposes, in which water from local streams was supposed to circulate. In fact, for most of its time, it was a stagnant nuisance despite attempts to clean it and keep its waters flowing. Sections were filled in at various points from the late eighteenth century onwards. Local ordinances forbade the deposition of any material in it and cattle were not supposed to enter its waters. At the south-west corner of the town wall a pool (the Butts Pool or Pwll-y-Butts) developed, probably used for watering cattle. The ditch and the pool were clearly sources of infection into the town's wells, the most famous incidence of which was the outbreak of 'Cowbridge fever' in 1853 from the polluted well in the grounds of the *Bear Hotel.*

Despite being a planned town the supply of drinking water did not figure in those plans; this was left to individual effort but which needed the controlling lord's permission. Formal supply came from relatively shallow artesian wells sunk into the underlying limestone. Wells were sunk largely thanks to communal effort, either paid for or given as part of service or under duress. Wells are of two forms: wells within the burgage plots of the better off tenants (they paid one shilling a year for their plots), from which water was raised in the traditional manner with buckets and ropes, and secondly, for those who could not afford to sink wells - the poorer cottagers - wells were sunk, probably by the town council or the lord of the town - located in public areas such as the sides of the main street. Eventually these were fitted with lever pumps. Both the wells and the pumps can still be found in the town. Today there are notable 'private' wells in Brinsons (Estate Agents), the *Duke of Wellington* public house, the yard of the *Bear Hotel* and the mayor's parlour in the Town Hall. They tend to be stone-lined with water at a depth of about four metres. In some dry seasons both wells and pumps would run dry but usually the one in the Town Hall was reliable. Pumps located in the street are significant reminders of days when water supply could not be taken for granted. There was no water supply to the town's Grammar School, not even for its boarders. One of the headmasters, Richard Williams, wrote when he first came to Cowbridge in 1919:

> The School was entirely dependent on wells and tanks and every drop of water had to be pumped or carried. There was one bath; but the only hot water was separated from it by the whole length of the buildings and one or two flights of stairs; everyone from the Head to Jones mi. . . had to bath in a small tub with a skimpy allowance of hot water! In the drought of 1921 we took short spells at the pumps throughout the day to get enough water to keep the kitchen boiler from bursting. (Iolo Davies, *'A Certaine Schoole'*, p. 277.)

A second source of water was the naturally occurring wells which were usually spring-like sources often walled in for protection and cleanliness. These often lay in open lands where the geology forced emissions to the surface. There are three significant ones locally: the Eye Well below Llanblethian Hill, Bowmans Well in open land near the Verlands housing estate and the Silver Well beyond the North Road, now in a private garden (fig. 3). These naturally occurring 'wells' were a major source of water for the less well-off citizens of Cowbridge but the labour involved in carrying water from sources to home was a considerable burden that usually fell on children and women.

Fig. 3: The Silver Well - one of the ancient public wells.
The present structure is probably 19th century. *Cowbridge History Society*.

Another significant source of water was the principal river, the River Thaw itself. Its regime until recently would have been very variable according to the season and the height of the water-table: bank full or in flood in the wet winters and often a mere trickle in the hotter summer season. Its course, too, varied over the centuries thanks to natural and human agencies. Its water was used for a variety of purposes - drinking (for people and cattle), for washing clothes, for industrial uses and for waste disposal, including waste from humans and from cattle on market days. Until the new bridge was opened in 1911 a chain pump for filling carts was to be found near the *Bridge Inn*. In parts of the town the banks of the river were used for the disposal of town waste, much of it ash and clinker from houses and local workshops and factories.

Numerous minor streams form part of the catchment of the Thaw, including the Factory Brook which flows from the neighbouring village of Llanblethian to the south. As its name suggests the latter was managed in such a way as to provide power for the woollen mills that flourished up to the early twentieth century, producing Welsh flannel and a kind of tweed. The principal one was the woollen factory of Llanblethian dating from the 1830s, but the site had been used as a mill – probably a fulling mill – from

Fig. 4: The woollen factory at Llanblethian powered by the Factory Brook.
The factory is the low-rise building to the right of the house.
Photo: Haydn Baynham. Cowbridge History Society.

the sixteenth century. The Thaw supported a flour mill from the mid fifteenth century to the twentieth, located beyond the South Gate in the town's walls at the appropriately named Town Mill Road, formerly Town Mill Lane. Another water mill within the locality was on the north side of the town in the Mill Field (now Druids Green).

Water was also important for Cowbridge's industries. Because the town was by-passed by Brunel's South Wales Railway in the 1850s, and only obtained a branch line in the 1860s, Cowbridge was not seen as a location for heavy industry that characterised so much of Victorian South Wales. Its industries were limited to those servicing local agriculture such as wood and metal working, forging and blacksmithing, and the production of food and drink for local consumption. Brewing was a major consumer of local water, drawn from artesian sources. It took something like twenty gallons of water to make one pint of beer. The first brewery, as opposed to an inn or beer house which brewed and sold its own beer, was located opposite Old Hall. Others included the important brewery near the bridge on the north side. Originally a malthouse, it began brewing in the 1880s, finally closing in 1955.

Health and sanitation

Medieval towns like Cowbridge were governed by agents of the controlling lords, in this case by the constable of Cardiff Castle (the *de facto* mayor) supported by a bailiff, acting for the lords of Glamorgan, the earls of Gloucester and later the Herberts, earls of Pembroke, who controlled this area of South Wales. Only slowly was power transferred to the local gentry, many of whom had town houses in Cowbridge or were principal tenants and who served as magistrates and justices of the peace. Although classed as a borough because of its chartered status there was no pretence at democracy; indeed, Cowbridge could probably be identified as a 'rotten borough'. The town was a source of rental income from the burgesses, from markets, fairs and tolls and for their burgage holdings. There was little concern for the general welfare of the population, including their living conditions.

The borough had certain powers over the common wells through its Court of Common Council established in 1460. This included control over drainage and the disposal of 'nuisances' such as material from the shambles and the markets held in the main street. Larger houses may have used a system of ash bins emptied by night-soil men but most domestic sewage came from privies usually located in the gardens of the cottages. It was disposed of in cesspits. From time to time the council employed an officer to enforce regulations. However, the general picture was one of considerable neglect in these areas. As a result contagion and infectious diseases quickly spread through the town, not helped by the fact that Cowbridge lay on the main road between Britain and Ireland, with many people passing through from all parts of the country. The Municipal Corporations Act of 1835 gave towns new powers but Cowbridge was considered too small to be included in the Act and the governance of the town remained in the hands of the same powerful families as it had been for centuries. They had little concern for the town's welfare. It was not until the establishment of local boards of health following the Public Health Act of 1848 and its amendment in 1858 that concern for local

Fig. 5: Cattle in the River Thaw near the centre of the town, c.1890.
The Brewery is on the left. *Cowbridge History Society.*

health was taken more seriously, especially after the national cholera outbreak of 1849. The state of Cowbridge became a public scandal following the typhoid epidemic in the town in 1853. These Acts did not impose a uniform system of local public health authorities; local councils were able to adopt them as and when they felt appropriate. In Cowbridge's case this was not until 1888 when, somewhat perversely, an urban sanitary district was declared under the control of the new, reformed borough council (elected under the terms of the charter granted by Queen Victoria in 1886), rather than a local board of health. This gave the town a certain independence of action regarding the regulations governing water supply, health and sewage which seemed to lead to a degree of neglect of their responsibilities.

By the 1881 census the population of the registration sub-division of Cowbridge had risen to 7,045 but in the built-up area it remained at 1,229, little more than fifty years before, housed in about 280 dwellings. A description of the town in 1889 noted that 'much of the small house property is of a wretched description, the houses being small and ill-ventilated, dilapidated, exceedingly damp with ground floors below the level of the unpaved and filth-sodden surface outside'.

In a report in the *Western Mail* in June 1873, the paper recorded improvement attendant upon new legislation; a medical officer of health and a sanitary inspector had been appointed and 'disagreeable nuisances have been attended to and remedied by the officers'. The flow of water in the town ditch - an 'open sewer' - was to be improved with its waters falling into the River Thaw but, dangerously, 'before that river passes through the town'! The water supply from wells was pronounced 'perfectly salubrious and well suited for all culinary purposes'. However, either things deteriorated quickly in the next decade or the earlier reports may have been somewhat careless with the truth, because in a report from John Spears for the Local Government Board in London in February 1889, he noted that the previous authority (the old borough council of Cowbridge) did nothing to alleviate the poor sanitary conditions in the town, yet the medical officer of health, Dr Bates, reported 'he could find nothing (of sanitary defects) worthy of mention' and that 'the district was the healthiest in the kingdom'. Spears also observed that 'much of the wretched house property in the town belongs directly or indirectly to town councillors'. These same councillors had recently agreed to the cattle market being moved from the ancient High Street location to a new site in the Butts, a good move to clean up the main thoroughfare and remove a major obstacle to traffic. However, the new market created fresh drainage problems because the main drain led into the Poplar Pool in the River Thaw next to the Poplars, then used as a day school. This was the notorious pool that was regularly blocked with sewage. No wonder the pupils complained of its offensiveness. In Church Street near the parish church and the Grammar School the corporation had recently sunk a cesspool measuring five feet square by four feet deep whose surface level was *above* the nearby houses! The inspector of nuisances appointed by the council was a dairyman who regularly went from cleaning out privies and cesspools back to his dairy!

Eventually they did appoint a new medical officer of health - the locally famous Dr Charles Booth Meller - at the miserly fee of £5 per annum which was later withdrawn but generously Meller carried out his civic duties on top of a busy practice for nothing. Spears reported that the council ignored the doctor's reports. Nevertheless, Meller constantly drew attention to the town's sanitary condition, including the fact that privies and related cesspools were in poor repair and a constant nuisance: 'they are very seldom emptied and their content is merely transferred from the cesspit into a hole dug in the garden within a few feet of the house'. Each year he examined the supply of water from the town's wells and found them wanting largely because the 'slop water' thrown into the streets by residents found its way into the underlying water-table. Given these conditions and the dreadful state of most houses, the epidemic of diphtheria in 1888 was hardly surprising. Annually, Dr Meller called upon the corporation to invest in proper sewers and a piped water supply, although he recognised that this would be 'attended by an enormous outlay'. It would be another forty years before there was piped water in Cowbridge.

Floods

Until recently floods were a regular occurrence in Cowbridge, a function of the town's low-lying position and the drainage pattern and characteristics of local catchments. Indeed, it calls into question the original decision of the town's founders in the thirteenth century in choosing such a location; clearly the access given by the old Roman road was more important than hydrology. Although it is difficult to generalise about the history of Britain's climate, it could have been that when the town was

Fig. 6: Cowbridge High Street flooded outside the Town Hall, 1947. *Western Mail.*

established this part of South Wales was still in the early medieval 'cold/dry' period when summers were frequently hot and winters very cold. Perhaps it was not until after the onset of the 'Little Ice Age' from about 1500 that precipitation and run-off increased. Certainly by the late eighteenth and early nineteenth centuries floods in Cowbridge were being frequently recorded. However, the records are rather patchy until the last century.

Why did Cowbridge and the neighbouring village of Llanblethian flood? The answer lies with a number of different catchments. The principal river, the Thaw, is short - only 21.4 km long. It rises to the north of the town in a series of places only slightly higher than Cowbridge but high enough to show an increase in rainfall totals. It emerges from springs in an area to the west of Llanharry, south of the M4 motorway, proceeds across Newton and Penlline Moors where further flows are added, before it enters a large, poorly-drained area of marshy land just between the by-pass and the High Street. It appears as a true, if small, urban river flowing through the town centre. In many ways the town is at a confluence of a number of smaller watercourses that join the Thaw, including streams from the north and, from the south-west, the more impressive Factory Brook which rises near Moorshead Farm. It is these that, historically, added to its propensity to flood. The rate of run-off is largely dependent upon the nature of the surface receiving the rain: if largely pasture the rain takes some time to percolate through the soil to the bedrock but if down to arable and regularly ploughed then run-off is much more rapid. The small streams to the north and west of the town have been intermittent thanks to the limestone geology but in periods of high precipitation have easily flooded, decanting large amounts of flood water into many parts of the town, notably the Athletic Ground, Eastgate and southwards into Llanblethian. The Factory Brook in making its way to the main channel of the Thaw frequently overflowed into the area around the Tŷ Mawr, while to the north of Cowbridge the marshy lands from just beyond the built-up area of the medieval town right out to beyond the by-pass and the site of the Comprehensive School were often in times past under the waters of a temporary lake.

Two years in (almost) recent memory stand out as bad years. The first was 1947 when much of the central area of the town was under water to a depth of one and a half to two feet (fig. 6). Besides homes and shops suffering, the High Street was inundated. Until the 1960s this formed part of the A48, the main highway between Cardiff and Swansea, itself part of the long-distance strategic route between Wales, Ireland and England and at all hours dense with industrial traffic; floods halted movements for most of the day. The second example dates from October and November 2000 when much of the village of Llanblethian was once again under water, residents having to retreat to their first-floor bedrooms. In Cowbridge town centre and in Westgate the same areas were flooded as in 1947 and many subsequent years. Much of the blame was put on a planning decision that, after an appeal, had permitted the development of housing on the floodplain to the north of the town, an area that historically - as we have shown - acted as a large sponge to slow down and absorb flood water from the River Thaw. Welsh Water, the Environment Agency, the Vale of Glamorgan Council and the Town Council had all objected to this development on the grounds of its likely effects on flooding. Clearly, at the appeal the planning inspector thought he knew best and the Middlegate housing estate was built on this high-risk land.

Residents also blamed the state of the town's storm water and sewage system, saying that it was 'Victorian', built for conditions a hundred years previously and not able to cope with the expansion of the town that had taken place from the 1960s onwards when many new housing estates were added to the medieval town plan.

Amongst other causes for flooding were obstructions in the river and stream channels. For example, the mill at Llanblethian had a sluice-gate that was often closed but should have been left open at time of high rainfall. But the miller, Harry Stone, had certain rights. After the great flood of 1947 he was persuaded to give up those rights and closed the mill. Near the centre of the town the river originally flowed under the old bridge, went under the main road and then emerged next to part of the High Street near the Limes. It is said that despite improvement to bridge and channel in 1911 this feature often led to the ponding up of water. It was not until a new channel was created in the floodplain alongside Mason's Yard and a new bridge built for the A48 in the early 1950s that this particular difficulty was mitigated. Unfortunately Cowbridge continued to flood.

The cost, human and economic, of these frequent flooding events eventually persuaded the Environment Agency - the successor to various river authorities - to develop a scheme to alleviate Cowbridge and Llanblethian's woes.

It has been calculated that, on average today, it can cost more than £28,000 per household to clean up after a flood, not to mention the personal distress it causes. After centuries of such fairly regular flooding in Cowbridge the Welsh Assembly Government agreed to fund an alleviation scheme at a cost of £1.3 million, to be built by Environment Agency Wales, for the town and its neighbouring village of Llanblethian. Largely completed in December 2006 it was designed to provide a measure of protection for residents and commercial properties, considered to be at risk from a one-in-a-hundred-year flood event. It involved the construction of an earth embankment dam and a fifty-metre-long reinforced concrete flood control structure on the floodplain of the River Thaw to be built to the north of the town. This would divert flood flows on to the natural floodplain away from Cowbridge and Llanblethian. To facilitate construction of the structure, a 100-metre-long river diversion was required. This was constructed out of blockstone to provide a natural habitat for fish. The dam came under the control of the Reservoir Act and the environmental impact of the scheme was carefully considered; many features were constructed which have a positive effect on wildlife such as the creation of ponds and shallow areas to attract water birds and insects and the development of an environmental area to encourage native wild flowers and plant life.

Local people in the Vale of Glamorgan began to see the benefit of these flood defences almost at once, following excessive rainfall in the district in the winter of 2006-7. They successfully protected local homes and businesses that had suffered from flooding in the past. Heavy rainfall within the catchment would have probably flooded properties had the flood storage reservoir upstream of Cowbridge not been constructed.

Heavy rainfall within the River Thaw catchment would have probably flooded properties in the village of Llanblethian too had the flood storage reservoir upstream of Cowbridge not been constructed. The scheme was substantially completed just before this event during December 2006.

Despite these engineering solutions, parts of the west end of the town continue to flood in times of very heavy rainfall, when surface water readily flows off saturated fields that are mostly given over to pasture.

The river, environment and recreation

But the river was not only a dangerous nuisance, a place for waste disposal, a source of floods, it was also a place of recreation. Although never wide enough or deep enough for serious boating, sections were used by the Grammar School between the Poplars footbridge and the Town Mill in the days when the river was wider. (John Richards, *The Cowbridge Story,* p. 29.) It was used quite often for raft racing, part of the numerous town carnivals in the 1950s and 1960s. The fishing rights were regularly sold off to local clubs from the mid-nineteenth century onward but not for stretches in the town. As can be imagined the river there until the 1990s was too polluted and unlikely to support fish; more recently it has been stocked with trout. Downstream in Llanblethian, known to some in the early nineteenth century as 'Little Switzerland' but to Thomas Carlyle as 'the Welsh Paradise of Sleepy Hollow', John Sterling - later to become one of the Cambridge Apostles - probably fished its waters. He certainly recalled 'the mill-stream into which I once fell'.

> My home was built upon the slope of a hill, with a little orchard stretching down before it, and a garden rising behind. At a considerable distance beyond and beneath the orchard, a rivulet flowed through meadows and turned a mill. . . The path to

> [Cowbridge] lay across the rivulet and past the mill; from which point we could either journey through the fields below the old castle, and the wood which surrounded it, or along a road at the other side of the ruin, close to the gateway of which it passed. The former track led through two or three beautiful fields, the sylvan domain of the keep on one hand, and the brook on the other. . . the brook in which, despite of maid and mother, I waded by the hour. (Thomas Carlyle, *The Life of John Sterling*.)

Swimming in rivers was a pastime much enjoyed in the nineteenth century - think of the Oxford dons and Parson's Pleasure on the Cherwell, think of Rugby Schoolboys fighting to keep their rights to swim in the Avon. In Cowbridge the same kind of enthusiasm led to the demand for a swimming pool in the early twentieth century. The scheme was actively promoted in 1911 by the mayor of Cowbridge, David Tilley. The proposed site was on land held by the Dunraven Estate whose agent gave right of access. Half the cost was borne by E. H. Ebsworth of Llandough Castle, the remainder being raised locally and from the council. The pool measuring eighty feet by twenty-two was opened soon after. It was made by excavating a suitable section of the river channel to provide length and depth (fig. 7). Controlling the flow was a series of sluice-gates that could be raised and lowered by hand. A pavilion for changing was built alongside. A set of rules was published which stipulated that no one was allowed to swim without a costume and all those over fifteen were to wear an 'Oxford costume'; no soap was to be used in the water. The headmaster of the Grammar School, Richard Williams, recorded in his reminiscences in 1938 that 'bathing was extremely popular and several summer terms we did not miss a single day'. (Iolo Davies, p. 277.)

For nearly forty years the swimming bath provided schoolchildren and others with a facility for outdoor swimming - perhaps not the healthiest environment - and certainly one of the coldest even on the hottest day. It did not fall into disuse until the coming of municipal swimming pools in the post Second World War period. Unfortunately, Cowbridge was never chosen as a site for one of these - the nearest pools being in Llantrisant, Penarth and Llantwit Major - in spite of its pioneering efforts and fierce lobbying.

Fig. 7: The swimming baths constructed in 1911 out of a stretch of the River Thaw.
Cowbridge History Society.

From time to time the river has been used for less official recreational purposes. Scouts, Cadets and others have tried to build rafts and other craft from ropes, barrels and spars, often under competitive circumstances.

The meadows on either side of the river between Cowbridge and Llanblethian are still grazed by cattle as they have been for centuries but in today's environmentally conscious times the valley of the Thaw is seen as an important habitat for a variety of aquatic plants and creatures. It acts as a throughway for various species moving from coast to hills. Among birds, besides the ubiquitous mallards, teals and pintails, can be found kingfishers, herons, wintering egrets, geese, dippers and a variety of wagtails. Historically otters (*lutra lutra*) frequented the river and otter hounds were kept by local landowners for the sport of hunting them, usually setting out from the *Bear Hotel*; there were frequent kills. Arthur John, a member of a well known local family, recalled the otter hounds coming down from the Wye Valley in the 1920s: 'One day they would beat up the river to City and back; the next day they would go down river to Aberthaw and back' (*Cowbridge and District Remembered*, p. 73). Although there have been recent claims of sightings of these protected animals there is not a great deal of evidence for their return. (Biodiversity action reporting system.) On the other hand, the water vole, with the help of protective legislation, is making a comeback. One particular scheme involves a number of partners working closely with landowners adjacent to the river. In 2007 it began to identify remaining water vole populations on the river and link suitable habitats in the catchment; pond and wetland habitats were created. Other benefits of the project have involved fencing along the river, installing livestock drinking bays and assessing the need for American mink control. The insect populations appear to be thriving and in the quieter stretches the dragon fly (*odonata anisoptera*), the damselfly (*odonata zygoptera*) and the lesser and greater water-boatman (*Corixa punctata* and *Notonecta glauca* respectively) can be seen on still summer evenings. All of these species appear to indicate that the River Thaw is a relatively clean system able to support a range of biodiversity.

Piped water supply

During the late nineteenth and early twentieth centuries there were many calls for a piped water supply for Cowbridge. The annual county medical officer's reports constantly stressed the need for clean water. In 1906 a local paper reported that it was in 1896 - ten years previously - that Dr R. Bruce Low recommended as first and foremost the provision of a public supply of water:

> Some years ago, the Corporation called in an expert water engineer to advise them and several schemes have since been formulated, but none carried out. A few years ago, a joint water scheme for Cowbridge and neighbouring villages was suggested, but neither the Corporation nor the Cowbridge Rural District Council took much interest in it, and eventually it was allowed to drop. St Hilary, which adjoins Cowbridge, is much in need of a public supply. Undoubtedly a joint water scheme would be best for Cowbridge and the adjoining District. There is no system of sewerage provided. How different the schools and other public buildings and places would be if there had been a public water supply and a scheme of sewerage provided. The most pressing requirement of Cowbridge is a public water supply. (*Glamorgan Gazette*, 6 April 1906.)

There was resistance to this idea. In 1908, at a meeting of the Glamorgan Sanitary Committee, one of its members, T. W. David (who represented Cowbridge on the County Council), said that wells in the neighbourhood were certified as satisfactory. He urged that 'the residents should not have forced upon them a scheme of water supply which would mean an expense of 3s. or 4s. in the pound'. (*Glamorgan Gazette*, 11 September 1908.) There was no comment on the part of the committee. A clear link between water supply and sewage removal was well known. A year later the town's medical officer of health (Dr R. M. Moynan) reported:

> The analyses, throughout the year, of the waters from the different public sources show that the waters continue to be of an improved quality and fit for domestic purposes. I can but reiterate my remarks in my many reports. There is no sound drainage for Cowbridge, but so long as there is no public water supply it is not advisable, nor is it desirable to have such, for without a free and regular supply of water for flushing purposes drains, etc., would become a source of danger to the public health. An efficient public water supply is required, as well as an efficient drainage and sewage system. (*Glamorgan Gazette*, 11 March 1909.)

The same year the headmistress of the Intermediate School for Girls reported that the supply of water from the school's well had failed and that water had to be carried from one of the town wells and stored in tubs (*Glamorgan Gazette*, 23 July 1909). By 1912 a ratepayer was writing to the editor complaining of the lack of progress, with people having to carry water from the Silver Well across a swampy meadow.

It was not until as late as 1926 that piped water - water on tap - arrived in Cowbridge and district following the establishment of the Mid Glamorgan Water Board in 1921; even then, it was only connected to the new council houses. (S. Millman, 'A geographical study of Cowbridge'.) Water was pumped from the collecting area on Newton Moors and stored in a reservoir near Llanharry to give a constancy of flow. Within a decade a new source was added by connecting supplies from the upper sections of the Ogmore and Garw valleys. Piped supply had an immediate effect; for one thing, it enabled central heating to be installed in the Grammar School. (Iolo Davies, p. 280.) Retro-fitting water pipes into the medieval and ancient houses of Cowbridge was no easy task. In addition to mains being laid in the streets, supply to individual houses was something of a nightmare. Not all properties wanted this newfangled system in which water now had to be paid for. Many shortcuts and cost saving measures were taken by the town's landlords - most properties were rented - including laying pipes through a line of terraced houses rather than providing individual supplies. In the same way the extensions to the sewage system were also constructed in an haphazard way with minor additions grafted on to the core sewer that ran down the centre of the High Street. When properties were modernised decades later builders and architects had to struggle with these anomalies. Nonetheless, in terms of physical infrastructure it was the beginning of the modernisation of what had become in physical terms a rather dilapidated, backward town. As the town's population grew from the 1960s thanks to the building of new housing estates to the east and west of the old medieval town centre, so new supplies had to be found. This entailed additional mains from much further afield. This was the beginning of the reorganisation of the water supply industry into fewer and larger units.

When a series of Conservative governments were returned after 1979 one of their objectives was to privatise the water supply industry. In many parts of the U.K. this resulted in the foundation of huge multi-national corporations, often with ownership and headquarters overseas. In much of South Wales it was the American Western Power Distribution Company, an electricity network company who took over from the publicly owned suppliers. However, much of Wales was fortunate in being able to offer and sustain a not-for-profit alternative in Dŵr Cymru Welsh Water. Since 2001, this has been owned, financed and managed by Glas Cymru. Unique in the water and sewerage sector, Glas Cymru is a company limited by guarantee and as such has no shareholders. The company serves over three million people in 1.4 million homes and businesses with 828 million litres of water each day via 26,500 miles of water mains and sixty-six impounding reservoirs.

Water supply, electricity and a main drains sewage system, followed by the building of the by-pass to take the heavy traffic of the old A48 out of the town centre, together created a platform for the future growth of Cowbridge from the 1960s. However, any proposals to expand the town from the present day (2016) such as those to be found in the Local Development Plan of the Vale of Glamorgan for 2013-22 would necessitate considerable capital expenditure in water-based infrastructure, especially in the sewage system which appears to be at full capacity.

The town and its water environment saw few changes from the eighteenth century to the early nineteenth. Later, the construction of a replacement bridge to carry motorised traffic, the channelling of the river, the introduction of modern sewers and piped water and the building of the flood alleviation scheme all contributed to a healthier, safer town, helping to protect its nationally important medieval townscape. Today the River Thaw is something of a backwater with small children feeding stale bread to the numerous ducks as it flows quietly under the town bridge and through the local park - unaware of all these changes - out through the Three Fields below St Quentin's Castle to Llanblethian, on its way to the Bristol Channel at Aberthaw.

NOTE

This essay arose from an invitation to the Cowbridge Rotary Club from WaterAid UK to participate in their Big History Project, 2015, a nationwide exercise collecting information on aspects of the history of water in the variety of communities in Britain. Cowbridge Rotary Club asked the author to compile this outline history on their behalf. He was given complete freedom to express his own findings and ideas.

SOURCES

Alden, Jeff (ed.), *Cowbridge and District Remembered, 1900-1950* (Cowbridge Record Society, 2002).

Alden, Jeff, *How Well Do You Know Cowbridge?* (Cowbridge Record Society, 2005).

Carlyle, Thomas, *The Life of John Sterling* (London, 1851).

Davies, Iolo, *'A Certaine Schoole': a History of the Grammar School at Cowbridge* (Cowbridge, 1967).

Hopkin-James, L. J., *Old Cowbridge* (Cardiff, 1922).

James, Brian Ll. & Francis, David J., *Cowbridge and Llanblethian Past and Present* (Barry and Cowbridge, 1979).

Millman, Stacie, 'A geographical study of Cowbridge and the Vale of Glamorgan', Barry Teachers' Training College, unpublished student dissertation, 1926.

Richards, John, *The Cowbridge Story* (Bridgend, 1956).
Robinson, David M., *Cowbridge: the Archaeology and Topography of a Small Market Town* (Swansea, 1980).

Biodiversity action reporting system (2001-7): River Thaw otter survey. UKbars.defra.gov.uk/archive. Consulted 17 November 2014.

Dŵr Cymru:
http://www.dwrcymru.com/en/Company-Information/Glas-Cymru.aspx. Consulted 9 February 2015.

Glamorgan Gazette (various dates):
Welsh Newspapers online www.welshnewspapers.llgc.org.uk/
Consulted various dates 2014-5.

A WEALTHY COWBRIDGE SHOPKEEPER

By Jeff Alden and Betty Whyatt

Philip Riden's interesting little book, *Cowbridge Trades and Tradesmen, 1660-1750*, which was published in 1981, lists the contents of Catherine Bassett's shop in Cowbridge in 1707. He states that the inventory provides the best indication available from Cowbridge material of what a local mercer's shop contained. The total value of Mrs Bassett's haberdashery and textiles appears to be only £3 11s. 9d., possibly the remnants of a once bigger and more valuable stock.

But just over forty years later another inventory had to be made on the death in 1750 of John Vallance of Cowbridge, another mercer. This time the value of haberdashery and textiles in his shop was not far short of £1,000. (The total valuation in his inventory was over £1,500.) Thus Vallance was a very prosperous man, and his shop must have been a veritable emporium containing, in addition to his main stock as a mercer or draper, metals, snuff and tobacco. The many (more than 150) people - mostly local - who owed him money at the time of his death are meticulously recorded; did they owe for goods supplied, or could Vallance have included moneylending as one of his business interests?

At the time of writing this article (in 1999) the location of John Vallance's shop was not known. But with the discovery only a few years later of the burgage rentals for Cowbridge, among the Bute papers in the National Library of Wales, it became clear that he traded from 50 High Street (on the corner of Church Street), though he may have rented other premises to be used as warehouses. John Vallance's widow Jane (Wilkins) was still living at 50 High Street as late as 1773; by 1784 she was living in Eastgate, in a house which probably combined East Villa and the Armoury. Jane Vallance died in 1788 and was buried at St Mary Church, where her grandfather had been the rector.

We know a little more about the Vallances. Probably the first of the family to settle in Cowbridge was another John, also a mercer, who died in 1733 leaving the bulk of his estate to his nephew, the John of this article. There is a will but alas no inventory. John and Jane Vallance had several children; their daughter Jane is mentioned in William Thomas's diary as

50 High Street, Cowbridge, as it may have looked in the 18th century.
Royal Commission on the Ancient and Historical Monuments of Wales.

'the beauty of Wales' - courted by many suitors, she married in 1761 Thomas Blackwell, a customs officer in Bristol.

Leaving aside the family history, just consider the inventory. Even without understanding what all these materials and textiles were, marvel at the countries and place-names which suggest an extensive trade.

Selected items from the inventory of John Vallance's shop, 1750

24 yards of Broadshaggs at 2/6 a yard
44 yards of Broad Napp at 5/- a yard
119 yards of Bays at 10d. a yard
75 yards of Limoge at 1/- a yard
26 yards of Blanketting at 2/- a yard
112 yards of Flannel at 10d. a yard
308 yards of Broadcloth at 6/- a yard
112 yards of German serge & Narrow Cloth at 2/- a yard
76 yards of worsted & hair shaggs at 2/6 a yard

13 pieces of Duroyes at 10/- a piece
619 yards of Shallooms at 12d. a yard
679 yards of Camlets & worsted Damaskes at 6/- a yard
945 yards of Fustians & checks at 12d. a yard
7 cotten gown at 6/- a gown
770 yards of Chinease Berrin Crapes & Plads at 12d. a yard
7 Pieces & a half of Dowlas at 25/- a piece
93 yards of Broomsgrove Flaxen at 18d. a yard
3 pieces of Holland measuring 24 yards each at 3/2 a yard
95 yards of Irish Holland at 3/6 a yard
218 yards of Irish Sheeting at 10d. a yard
91 yards of Mushing at 3/- a yard
203 yards of Canvas at 6d. a yard
110 lb. of Wick Yarn at 6d. a lb.
3 dozen of hair cloths 00-12-00
30 lb. of Cotten woll at 1/6 a lb.
33 lb. of worsted at 20d. a lb.
3 lb. of Hemp 00-02-00
24 Shammey Skins at 10d. a skin
1 piece of Nankeen at 00-05-00
56 lb. of rope at 3d. a lb.
8 lb. of Wale Bone at 4/- a lb.
91 yards of Yellow Canvas, Brown Holland and Rusha Drabb at 14d. a yard
55 yards of Ticken at 16d. a yard
18 yards of Coarse Ticken at 8d. a yard
1 Bed and Boulster of Flanders Ticken 00-18-00
18 ells of Russha Cloth at 6d. a ell
20 yards of Buckram & Glazed Linnen at 9d. a yard
47 yards of Russha hempton at 2½d. a yard

The article in the last Newsletter asked for information on the nature and uses of the materials and textiles listed in the 1750 inventory of John Vallance's shop. I am indebted to Mrs Betty Whyatt of Llanblethian for her prompt response, which has solved many of the problems.

'Most of the fabrics are pretty straightforward and of a practical nature. As most clothing would have been lined, many of the fabrics are for that purpose. The Wale Bone (whalebone) speaks for itself, while many of the corsets and stomachers would have had Fustian in them, as well as canvas.

'The 770 yards of Chinease Berrin Crapes and Plads have me guessing. This may be some slight evidence that the extravagant mid-eighteenth-century fashions had had some influence on South Wales - but at 12d. a yard it was hardly expensive!

'Some specific details:

Duroy: a coarse woollen West of England cloth. There is a reference in a 1722 *London Gazette* to someone 'wearing a duroy coat and waistcoat'.

Fustian: originally produced at Fustal (Cairo) in Egypt. A fabric having a linen warp and a thick twilled cotton weft, which is cut one side, showing a low pile. In the thirteenth century St Paul's Cathedral had a 'white chasuble [vestment] of fustian'.

Nankeen: a cotton cloth of yellowish-brown colour, originally made in Nanking in China. It was usually used for breeches or trousers.

Dowlas: a coarse linen used chiefly for shirts, smocks, etc. It was poor country wear.

Shagg: a napped fabric, usually of rough wool, sometimes used for linings.

Broadcloth: a fine woollen cloth of plain weave. [One of the more expensive cloths in the inventory].

Serge: a loosely woven twilled worsted. Many varieties were imported with the names of origin distorted - for example, Serge de Nimes became known as 'Denim'.

Holland: a kind of linen, used especially for furnishing. Brewer's *Dictionary of Phrase and Fable* states that it is so called because it used to be sent to Holland to be bleached.

Shalloom: a light twill-weave woollen fabric, used chiefly for coat linings, and originally made in Chalons sur Marne, from which it derived its name.

Camlet: a fine cloth made of goat's hair, taking its name from the Arabic for the Angora goat.

Damask: a reversible fabric, usually silk or linen, with a pattern woven into it. Originally from Damascus.

Drabb: a fabric of a dull grey or brown colour.

'Some of the other words are by modern standards misspelled. Bays is probably baize; Mushing could well be muslin; Ticken is ticking. Crapes and plads are, of course, crepes and plaids'.

So we have sorted out the origins and meanings of most of the fabrics. Some are still a puzzle - for instance, was Bromsgrove (Worcestershire) a centre of the British linen industry? ('Broomsgrove Flaxen at 18d. a yard'.) In addition, judging by the astonishing length of materials - Vallance had miles and miles of the stuff, if you add it all up - was he a wholesaler, or an importer, rather than just a simple shopkeeper? The Society would love to know if any reader can come up with more information about John Vallance's business. The inventory would make a very interesting research project for somebody.

SOURCES

John Vallance's inventory is in the National Library of Wales, LL/1750/42. A complete transcript is printed in Peter Bowen (ed.), *Shopkeepers and Tradesmen in Cardiff and the Vale* (Cardiff, 2004), pp. 109-18.

Alden, Jeff (ed.), *Cowbridge: Buildings and People* (Cowbridge Record Society, 1999).

Denning, R. T. W. (ed.), *The Diary of William Thomas 1762-1795* (Cardiff, South Wales Record Society, 1995).

Riden, Philip, *Cowbridge Trades and Tradesmen, 1660-1750* (Cardiff, 1981).

HANGINGS ON THE STALLING DOWN

By Brian James

In 1768 the judges decided to transfer the Court of Great Sessions for the county of Glamorgan from its traditional meeting place in Cardiff to the town hall in Cowbridge. (That is, the old guildhall which stood in the middle of the High Street, near its junction with Church Street.) According to the diarist William Thomas the judges had been affronted in some way in Cardiff. Over the next fifteen years or so the town council of Cowbridge spent substantial sums of money in repairing and enlarging the building to accommodate the court. It was a big thing for Cowbridge to play host to the Sessions because they brought large numbers of people and their money into the town. The Sessions were held twice a year, in April and August.

But the bonanza only lasted twenty years. From 1788 the Sessions were back in Cardiff. There is no clear explanation of why, though there was certainly much debate at the time about which town was the most convenient.

The point is that it was only the judges in the Great Sessions (later called the Assizes) who had the power to pass a sentence of death. And the sentences were carried out on the nearest open space, which in the case of Cowbridge was the Stalling Down. Hangings took place there only during that period of twenty years - 1768 to 1787 - when the Great Sessions were held in Cowbridge.

As is well known, laws in the eighteenth century were very severe; many crimes that would today seem relatively trivial carried the death penalty. Apart from murder and treason, many forms of housebreaking, burglary and common theft were capital offences if the property stolen was worth more than five shillings. Highway robbery, wrecking (a favourite pastime along the coast of the Vale), counterfeiting and forgery, and rioting were also crimes for which a person might be hanged. In practice, however, the courts were surprisingly sympathetic towards petty criminals and juries might refuse to find someone guilty if the likely punishment seemed disproportionate to the offence. Occasionally goods might be valued at 4s.11d. to avoid the capital charge of grand larceny. And even when the jury convicted and the judge passed the death sentence, in a majority of cases the penalty was commuted from hanging to transportation to the colonies.

In general it was only convicted murderers who could expect no mercy. And following death on the gallows, the body of a murderer would be displayed in a public place, near the scene of the crime, suspended from a gibbet, enclosed within an iron frame. The judge also had the power to allow surgeons to take the corpses of murderers for dissection, but there is no evidence that this ever happened in eighteenth-century Glamorgan.

Only six people (all of them men) were executed by hanging during those twenty years that the Great Sessions were held in Cowbridge. At least ten others were condemned and then reprieved. More than thirty prisoners left Cowbridge on their way to exile and hard labour in the colonies, in North America or the West Indies. (The first convict fleet set sail for Australia in 1787.) For minor offences (called misdemeanours) the common punishments were physical, either branding or whipping.

The courts were usually kept quite busy, even though Glamorgan was then a mainly rural county with a population of no more than about 60,000. There were frequent cases of murder, manslaughter and infanticide. Time and again young women were brought before the court charged with killing their illegitimate babies. But in all the cases mentioned by William Thomas in his diary the women were acquitted. Such cases were difficult to prove perhaps, and perhaps sympathetic juries were moved to give the unfortunate young women the benefit of the doubt. There was only one really local murder, that of Elizabeth William of Aberthin in January 1779. Her burial is recorded in the Llanblethian parish register. William John of Aberthin was tried at the April Sessions for her murder, and was acquitted. No further information about this crime has been preserved.

There is, however, some information about each of the six men who were hanged on the Stalling Down and about the crimes that they had committed. But first of all, we can offer some account of the way in which they met their end.

Many people seem to believe that the gallows stood on the highest point of the Stalling Down, where the clump of trees is. Sometimes it is even suggested that prisoners were hanged from a branch of one of the trees. None of this is true. It is not even certain if there were any trees there in the eighteenth century. (The famous clump was probably planted by the Rev. J. M. Traherne to commemorate the Battle of

Waterloo, 1815.) The actual site of the gallows was on lower ground close to Hollybush Farm, so the crowds that came to see an execution gathered on the rising ground to the north and the south of the track that runs across to Hollybush. Hopkin-James, in his *Old Cowbridge* (p. 58), wrote that 'felons were hanged on Stalling Down, according to tradition, on the Aberthun (Hollybush) side on a spot where the fern never grows'. George Yates's map of Glamorgan, published in 1799, marks the gallows roughly there, though no one can say precisely where it stood. It was evidently a permanent structure of two upright posts and a crosspiece, something like modern soccer goalposts; the crosspiece would have to have been rather higher off the ground, presumably. The gallows remained in place long after it had ceased to be used; the tradition was that the timber posts were eventually stolen to make furniture.

The prisoner - his arms and legs tied and with the noose already around his neck - was conveyed up from Cowbridge to the place of execution in a cart or tumbril, accompanied by a large crowd of people. A clergyman (probably the sheriff's chaplain) rode in the cart with the prisoner and would try to obtain a confession; he would read prayers and part of the burial service. The cart made its slow, lumbering journey up to the summit of the Stalling Down, then turned into the track that runs along the side of the Down, and finally into the track towards Hollybush. It would come to a halt under the gallows; the rope would be tied to the crosspiece and, at the command of the sheriff (who was in charge of proceedings), horse and cart would move forward leaving the prisoner suspended. Since there would not have been much of a 'drop', death would result from strangulation and not from the breaking of the neck. It would not therefore be instantaneous - far from it. The gradually weakening struggles and writhings of the body and the facial contortions of the victim were, of course, very much part of the spectacle that the crowd had assembled to watch. There is no evidence, but one may suspect that many of the spectators would be wagering money on how long it took the prisoner to die.

Now for something about each of the six men who were hanged on the Stalling Down between 1768 and 1787. The information that exists is far short of providing complete biographies; the facts mostly come from the official record of the Court of Great Sessions, from the ever useful diary of William Thomas and from contemporary newspaper reports.

1. Henry Thomas of Ystradgynlais in Breconshire was hanged in April 1770 for the murder of Watkin Thomas of Boverton, who was travelling near Pontardawe in the Swansea Valley. While drinking together in an alehouse, Henry noticed that Watkin had a great deal of money in his purse. (It turned out to be as much as fifty shillings.) Henry Thomas is described in the official record as a labourer, but the diary makes it clear that he had been until recently a servant employed by the squire of Ynyscedwyn; possibly he had had no regular work since leaving the squire's service. He was twenty-one or twenty-two years old. His corpse was subsequently hung on a gibbet, presumably somewhere in the west of the county near where the crime had been committed.

2. Thomas Arthur of Lisvane, a labourer, was hanged in August 1778 for the murder of Joan Watkin of Cyncoed, near Cardiff, a farmer's widow aged seventy-five. He was twenty. From William Thomas's account it seems that the murder was committed in the course of a burglary at the Widow Watkin's farmhouse. We are told that Thomas Arthur stole 'but a trifle from her, two yards of swanskin [which was a kind of flannel], a bottle of liquor etc'. His body was hung on a gibbet set up on the Great Heath, perhaps near the present-day public house where the Merthyr and Caerphilly roads meet, in north Cardiff.

3. John Thomas Harry of Eglwysilan, a cobbler, was hanged in May 1786. There were three indictments against him at his trial: one for stealing a beaver coat the property of Richard Thomas; two, for stealing a silver watch the property of William David; three, for a burglary which is not specified in the record. With so many charges proved against him, the judge doubtless decided that an example had to be made of John Thomas Harry - thieves were almost routinely reprieved, but in this case the ultimate punishment was exacted. This is what William Thomas wrote in his diary:

> Was hanged on Stalling Down John Thomas Harry, about 45 years old, that dreadful thief, and his corpse was set in a coffin and carried to be buried to Eglwys Ilan, and great was the crowd that came to see his death.

This execution was reported in the *Bristol Journal* (there were no newspapers published in South Wales at the time). From this we learn that two clergymen had been in the cart with the prisoner and they 'spared no pains to bring him sensible of his unhappy situation. He made a confession of his guilt and of sundry crimes committed by him for many years back, and appeared to die penitent'.

John Thomas Harry seems to have been the only one of the six who had pursued a life of crime, and it was probably for this reason that his sentence was not commuted.

4. Hopkin Thomas alias Bowen, a labourer from Llangyfelach, was found guilty on two counts - stealing a gelding belonging to William Rees and stealing a mare belonging to William Jenkin. The theft of horses and livestock was common in the county, so perhaps the judge did not recommend a reprieve as a warning to others, and the man was hanged in August 1786. He was twenty-two. According to William Thomas the corpse was buried at St Hilary (the nearest churchyard), but there is no record of this in the parish register, probably because the parish clergyman would not have read the burial service.

It is a notable fact that at the same court one Edward William, a labourer of Newport in Monmouthshire, was condemned for stealing two oxen the property of Thomas George. But his sentence was commuted to transportation for life. He died on the voyage to Botany Bay in 1789.

5 and 6. Two men were hanged on 20 April 1787, the last to die on the Stalling Down gallows.

William Owen of Merthyr Tydfil, a labourer, was found guilty of murdering his lover, Mary Harris, a servant in the household of Mr Bacon of Merthyr, the ironmaster, by stabbing her with a penknife. He was about twenty-three.

Cornelius Gordon of Llanrhidian, yeoman, was found guilty of killing his wife, Mary (Bevan), by striking her with a spade as they worked together in the garden of their farmhouse. Cornelius was thirty-seven.

Mary Harris was killed on 1 April and Mary Gordon on 4 April. Their murderers were tried in the Sessions on 14 April and executed on 20 April 'before the judges left the town of Cowbridge'. It had all happened in less than three weeks. 'A dismal tragedy', commented William Thomas in his diary. Eighteenth-century justice could be very swift.

The execution of Cornelius Gordon was still remembered in the neighbourhood of Cowbridge well over a hundred years later. In 1922 Hopkin-James noted in his *Old Cowbridge* (p. 59): 'According to local tradition, the last person to be hanged there was a yeoman from Gower of the name of Gordon'. But no details of the event could be recalled by that date. However, around 1860 David Jones of Wallington talked to an old lady at St Mary Church, Mrs Ann Howe, who had been present on the Stalling Down on that day in April 1787; she was then a young girl of ten or eleven years of age. The occasion and the man's name remained in her mind throughout her long life, but nothing else that she remembered about it seems right. The reality had faded to be replaced by myth or a figment of the imagination. 'The whole Down trembled at the instant he was hanged as with an earthquake', she told David Jones. She also said that she had stood by Cornelius's mother who, with other members of his family, had brought a coffin to take the body back to Gower for burial. This seems unusual to say the least. The record is unfortunately not clear in this instance, but the law *was* clear that a murderer could not be buried but his corpse had to be hung in chains on a gibbet. Yet, could the Gordon family have had sufficient influence to obtain this favour? For everyone at that time regarded the denial of burial as something abhorrent, perhaps even more shameful than execution itself.

The point is that Cornelius Gordon (sometimes Gorton) was different from the other victims of the law who suffered on the Stalling Down - he had social status. He belonged to one of the most prominent families on the Gower Peninsula. A relative, Richard Gordon of Burry Green, had even been the sheriff of Glamorgan in 1770. This is almost certainly why *his* name was remembered for so long, and why the young labourer from Merthyr, William Owen, who was hanged alongside him, was forgotten. Mrs Howe remembered her social equal, but forgot the labourer.

Public executions were not abolished until 1868. After 1788 in Glamorgan they took place on the Little Heath, between Cardiff and Roath, and after about 1830 on a platform in front of the county gaol in St Mary Street, where the famous Dic Penderyn was hanged in 1831 for his supposed part in the Merthyr Rising. (The covered market was built on the site after the gaol was moved to its present location.)

SOURCES

National Library of Wales, Great Sessions Records. Glamorgan, Brecon & Radnor: The Black Book.

Denning, R. T. W. (ed.), *The Diary of William Thomas. . . 1762-1795* (Cardiff, South Wales Record Society, 1995).
Evans, Gill, 'Cornelius Gordon 1750-1787', *Glamorgan Family History Society Journal,* 94 (June 2009), pp. 10-13.
Hopkin-James, L. J., *Old Cowbridge* (Cardiff, 1922).
Howell, David W., *The Rural Poor in Eighteenth-century Wales* (Cardiff, University of Wales Press, 2000), chapter 10 on crime.

OLD HALL, COWBRIDGE

By Jeff Alden

Have you ever considered what was the purpose of the stonework which is outlined in the paved area outside Old Hall - between the Community College and the walls which formed the facade of the eighteenth-century building? It looks like this:

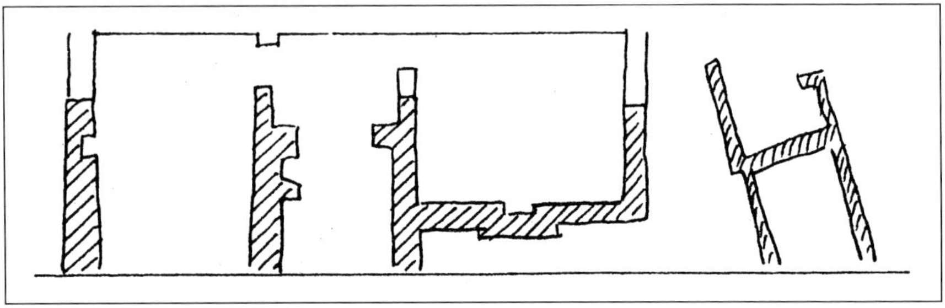

Fig. 1: Outline of stonework outside Old Hall.

The building - which had been used by the Grammar School - was deemed to be unsafe in 1964. The architect's report in 1970 confirmed evidence of death-watch beetle, powder-dust beetle and woodworm, with wet and dry rot throughout the building. There was cracking and spoiling of stonework particularly on the garden front; major structural cracking indicating movement of the garden elevation wall; the roof structure of the main block was unsafe. 'The building is in a very poor state'. So only the lower part of the exterior wall on the garden side was preserved, and the internal walls in that part of the building were demolished - but the bases of the walls and the outlines of the rooms are what we see today.

This article is an attempt to trace the development of the house from the time of its construction in the seventeenth century, and to show the changing uses to which the rooms were put.

In the early house, the Royal Commission on the Ancient and Historical Monuments of Wales envisage the main room - the hall - as being on the left-hand side of the building when looked at from the street, i.e. next to where Barclays Bank is today (but then separated from the bank building by a narrow passage. There is still one small seventeenth-century

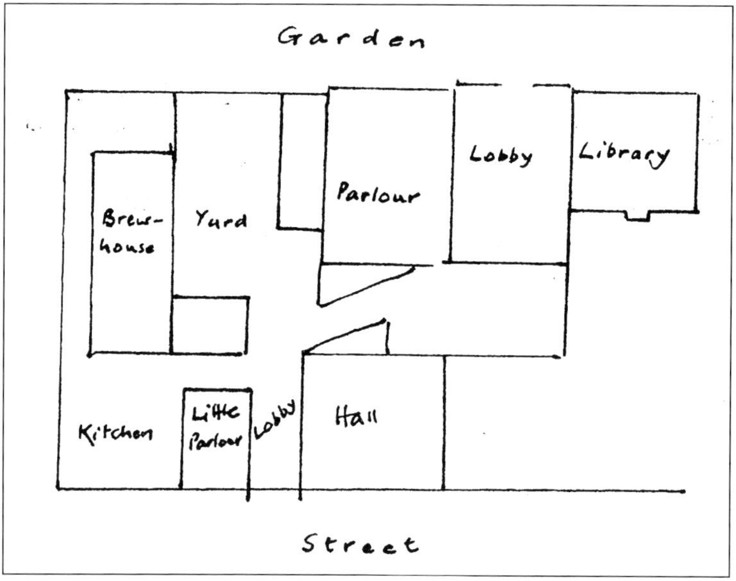

Fig. 2: Ground floor in the eighteenth century.

Fig. 3: Nineteenth-century watercolour of the garden front of Old Hall.
Cowbridge History Society.

window visible in the wall overlooking the passage). There were other rooms on the street side and behind; but by the mid-eighteenth century the Edmondes family (who had purchased the house in the 1740s) had added a suite of rooms with a classical frontage and Venetian windows on the garden side of the building. In an inventory of 1762, done for John Edmondes, we find a library, hall and two parlours, a well-equipped kitchen and brewhouse, and ten bedrooms (but only three of which could be considered to be elaborately furnished, the remainder presumably being for the children and the servants). Of interest in the two lobbies were two orange trees in tubs and a Sedan or Bath chair - which gives us an idea of life in Cowbridge at that time. There were lots of maps, prints and pictures on the walls, curtains on the windows of the main rooms and enough good furniture and china to show that this was the home of a family which was comfortably well off. We can also make a pretty good stab at working out which room was which.

A watercolour of the middle of the nineteenth century shows the classical frontage overlooking a pleasant garden, with croquet hoops on the lawn in front of the building (no pond or sunken garden then). The Archdeacon's diaries, to which I made reference in an earlier Newsletter [and the subject of a talk to the Cowbridge Record Society printed in *Echoes of Old Cowbridge*], describe Archdeacon Edmondes playing croquet with his father, the Rev. Thomas Edmondes, on summer afternoons on the lawn.

A photograph taken later in the century shows the street side of Old Hall, with a small porch, oriel window above, a doorway on the left (Barclays) side of the building, all separated from the High Street by a low, ornate fence linking impressive stone pillars. Study of the census enumerators' books for 1861 and 1881, together with plans of the building before the changes near the turn of the century, indicate that not all of the building was occupied by the Edmondes family. It appears that the Stockwoods of Woodstock House (opposite Old Hall) used the right-hand side as a sort of overspill for younger unmarried members of their family. It is likely that this part of the building is an early nineteenth-century addition to the main block. The stables beyond (where the flats are today) housed a variety of vehicles - carriages, gigs and dog carts, as well as the horses.

After the death of the Rev. Thomas Edmondes in 1892 came a significant rebuild of the street frontage of Old Hall in a heavy Tudor style, the new porch being faced with stone, as was the north-west gable in that

Fig. 4: Photograph of the street frontage of Old Hall before the alterations of c.1900. *Cowbridge History Society*.

part of the building which had been occupied by the Stockwoods. The major changes internally were the addition of a study and billiard room, with bedrooms above, in this 'new' part of the building.

The Edmondes family continued to live in Old Hall until about 1930; but then came a major change.

The increase in the number of pupils at the Grammar School made it essential that more classrooms were provided, and so the school moved into Old Hall in January 1932. Initially a new physics laboratory, an extra staff room and a changing room were provided. However, the *Bovian* of December 1933 recorded 'the migration of IIIA to the upper region of Old Hall, and IIIA in its turn has caused the banishment of IIIB to the old nursery. We hope this is in no wise a reflection on the work of the Lower Third, and we are ready to believe that those pictorial representations of nursery rhymes, that do so much to break the monotonous mural expanses of green, have been considered unworthy of notice by at least one member of the form'. Eventually five form rooms, the physics lab., a music room and the library on the ground floor were in use. During the War, blast walls were erected on the garden side in front of the two ground floor rooms; otherwise the garden remained peaceful and beautiful, with a sunken garden where the lily pond is today, a grass tennis court where the

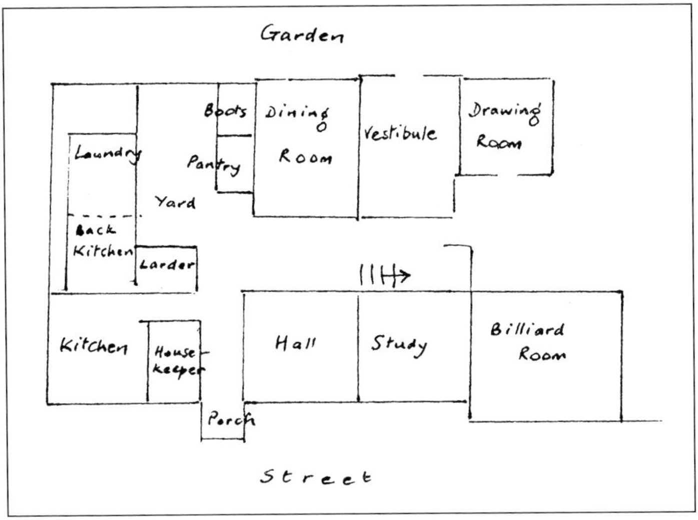

Fig. 5: Ground floor in the early twentieth century.

public library building is, and large trees - including copper beech, yew, monkey puzzle, mulberry and walnut. (Beyond the town wall, where the car-park now stands, was Mr Pratt's orchard, full of apple trees with lovely red, juicy apples.)

Adrian Trotman, who was a pupil of the school in the 1940s, has worked out the plan for me, and has given me a lot of information about the building at that time - and later, when he came back to teach there. Most of the left-hand side (earlier the kitchen, larder and wash-house, with servants' quarters above) was occupied by Mr Penny, the groundsman and caretaker. On the ground floor, to the right of the porch on the street side, the former hall was used as a cloakroom, and was designated the air-raid shelter in wartime. Next to it was the staff room, which had a wonderful carved mantelpiece (reputed to have been by Grinling Gibbons) and in the adjacent IIIA classroom was a stag's head on the wall - a souvenir of its days as a billiard room - and fine Delft tiles around the stove. There were also Delft tiles in the staff lavatory. The other main room on the ground floor, the library, had wall-to-wall, floor-to-ceiling shelves, white painted and well equipped with books; the room was mainly used for Classics teaching. Upstairs, the physics laboratory occupied the room which includes the projection over the porch.

The stable yard was, certainly in the time of Mr Idwal Rees, used to garage the headmaster's car, and some of the outbuildings were used to store the many and varied props for the school play productions in the Town Hall, or earlier in the Pavilion cinema.

So if we go back to the walls outlined in the paving, there are in effect three main rooms shown. In the time of the school they were IVA classroom, the entrance hallway and the library; in the nineteenth- and twentieth-century home of the Edmondes family they were dining-room, vestibule and drawing-room; in the eighteenth century the great parlour, lobby and library. Before that, Old Hall was a smaller house, and these rooms did not exist! In the present-day Community College, the only room which preserves some fragment of the earliest house is the large room upstairs, where the massive (probably seventeenth-century) fireplace is a prominent feature.

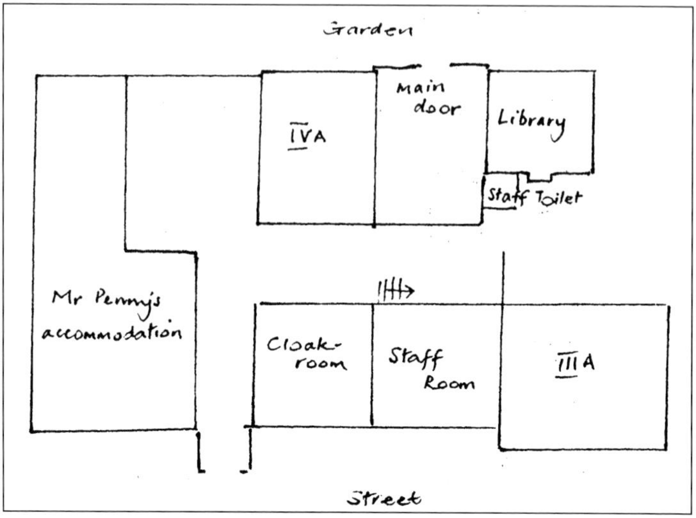

Figs. 6: Ground floor when in use by the Grammar School in the mid-twentieth century.

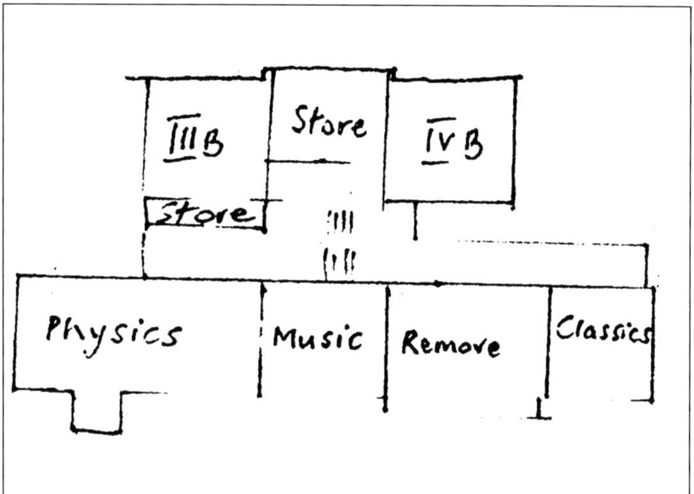

Figs. 7: First floor when in use by the Grammar School in the mid-twentieth century.

SOURCES

The Old Hall inventory of 1762 is in the Glamorgan Archives, DEd 450.

Alden, Jeff, 'The Edmondes diaries', in *Echoes of Old Cowbridge* (Cowbridge Record Society, 2011), pp. 77-85.
Davies, Iolo, *'A Certaine Schoole': a History of the Grammar School. . .* (Cowbridge, 1967).
Llantwit Major and Cowbridge (Aberystwyth, Royal Commission on Ancient and Historical Monuments of Wales, 1989).
Thomas, Hilary M. (ed.), *Historic Gardens of the Vale of Glamorgan* (Welsh Historic Gardens Trust, South and Mid Glamorgan Branch, 2007), pp. 36-9.

LLANBLETHIAN COTTAGE INVENTORY

By Luke Millar

The transcript of the Llanblethian Cottage inventory of 1819 is accompanied by a glossary and notes on those items which might be unfamiliar or require explanation to the general reader. Of several other gentry house inventories of roughly the same period and from this area, those from Old Hall, Cowbridge, of 1762 and 1778 have been chosen mainly for comparison, because some things had changed considerably during the intervening forty years, and others notably had not.

As one might expect, the furniture was of different periods and styles, although the minimal description made by the inventory takers often obscures such changes. So a 'mahogany chair' could describe two very different items, but the 'fancy chairs' in 1819 are very much nineteenth-century things, as is the 'sofa table', not made before about 1790.

There are no particular differences in the domestic appliances, mainly trivial items of daily life which have a fascination for us because they seem to put us in touch with the intimate details of people's lives, which thereby seem more real to us. Some such things are specified in detail, such as various kinds of trays. Others, such as brewing equipment and the methods one can deduce from them, would repay comparison with a wide range of inventories at different social levels.

In general, the inventory covers a comprehensive range of furniture and equipment, although it is rather short on carpets and curtains and entirely lacking tableware and silver. Curtains in particular were fashion items at the time, often elaborately draped on pole cornices or 'French rods', with cord pulls. Presumably all these things were retained by the Courtenays and taken with them to their next place of residence (perhaps Buckland, Devon).

[Mr Millar transcribed the following inventory retaining the spelling of the original. Ed.]

An Inventory of Household Furniture etc. the property of C. Courtnay Esq. sold by auction at Llanblethian on Wednesday the 4th day of August 1819 by John Awbrey Auctioneer

1.	6 Pickling jars	0.4.6
2.	2 Tin coffee pots	0.1.3
3.	Coffee mill	0.4.3
4.	Pair of iron candlesticks	0.0.8
5.	Tin candlestick, snuffers & stand	0.1.2
6.	Gridiron & 2 forks	0.6.0
7.	Iron footman	0.10.6
8.	Iron boiler	0.5.0
9.	Do.Do.	0.5.0
10.	Iron digester	0.5.0
11.	2 iron saucepans	0.4.0
12.	Bell mettle kettle	0.4.0
13.	Tin saucepan and copper tea kettle	0.4.0
14.	Frying pan dripping pan & 2 skimmers	0.5.0
15.	Japan cannister & 1 Do.	0.4.6
16.	Cheese bonnet & cullinder	0.3.6
17.	3 Flat irons & stand	0.3.0
18.	Iron box & stand	0.3.0
19.	Brass warming pan	0.6.0
20.	Steelyard	0.6.0
21.	2 Knife trays	0.1.0
22.	2 Japan waiters	0.0.6
23.	6 table mats	0.2.6
24.	Plate rack	0.11.0
25.	Deal kitchen table	0.18.0
26.	6 Kitchen chairs	0.18.0
27.	1 Clothes horse	0.11.0
28.	3 Green chairs	0.13.0
29.	2 elbow Do.	0.9.6
30.	Barometer	1.2.0
31.	6 elbow chairs	1.13.0
32.	Mahy. card table	1.2.0
33.	Pier looking glass	1.10.0
34.	Sett of fire irons, fender & hearth brush	0.7.6

35.	Sett of mahy tables	3.3.0
36.	Mahy card table	1.11.6
37.	Do. work table	0.12.0
38.	Do. celeret	0.15.0
39.	Do. Sofa	4.4.0
40.	Pair of curtains	0.7.0
41.	Piece of carpeting	0.11.0
42.	8 rush botom chairs	1.15.0
43.	A Telescope	5.0.0
44.	Sett of fire irons, fender & hearth brush	0.8.0
45.	1 eight day clock	7.7.0
46.	2 clothes flasks	0.6.0
47.	Beech tent bedstead	2.6.0
48.	Bed wt.76 lb. @ 1/6	5.14.0
49.	Pair of blankets	0.10.6
50.	Mahy. Chest of drawers	3.13.6
51.	Wash hand stand basin & ewer	0.13.0
53.	Deal dressing table	0.4.6
54.	2 Fancy chairs	0.4.0
55.	Sett of fire irons, fender & hearth brush	0.6.0
56.	Bed wt.102 lb. @ 1/7 lb.	8.1.6
57.	Do. Do.38 lb. @ 1/6	2.17.0
58.	Pair of blanketts	1.6.0
59.	Bedside carpet	0 9.0
60.	Do.Do.	0.12.0
61.	Mahy. bidet	0.6.0
62.	Do. night stool	0.14.0
63.	3 fancy chairs	0.7.0
64.	Dressing table	0.14.0
65.	3 Fancy chairs	0.7.0
66.	Bootjack & clothes horse	0.3.0
67.	Basin & ewer	0.1.6
68.	Bedstead & furniture	3.3.0
69.	Bed wt. 60 lb. @ 1/10	5.16.0
70.	Pair of blankets	1.6.0
71.	Mahy. chest of drawers	2.12.6
72.	Deal dressing table	0.13.0
73.	Mahy. night stool	0.13.0

74. 2 Fancy chairs	0.4.0
75. Wash hand stand, basin & ewer	0.7.0
76. Bedstead	0.7.6
77. 6 fancy chairs	1.1.0
78. Oak bedstead	0.10.6
79. 1 Table	0.2.0
80. Dinner service of ware	1.8.0
81. Wooden clock	0.8.0
82. Toasting screen	0.6.6
83. Plate warmer	0.4.9
84. Coffee oven(?)	0.8.0
85. Dinner tray	0.6.0
86. 5 Baskets	0.8.6
87. Coal skuttle and box	0.5.0
88. Plate basket and bellows	0.7.0
89. Chamber bucket & duster	0.4.0
90. 3 Candlesticks &c.	0.3.0
91. Pewter dish & 2 plates	0.2.0
92. Coat jack	0.1.6
93. Stable bucket & 2 pails	0.6.3
94. 4 doz. of bottles	0.8.8
95. 4 doz. of Do.	0.8.8
96. 4 doz. of Do.	0.8.8
97. Bottle rack	0.5.6
98. Chopping board & knives	0.2.6
99. Stool and chairs	0.2.0
100. Vat	0.14.0
101. Cooler	0.4.6
102. 2 tubs	0.6.0
103. Funnel, mashing stick & cross stick	0.2.0
104. Wheelbarrow	0.10.0
105. Large screen	0.14.0
106. Handbarrow	0.4.0
107. Watering pot	0.2.6
108. Dog house	0.12.0
109. Flower stand	0.4.6
110. Cucumber frame	2.2.0
111. Half barrel	0.8.0

112. Do. Do.	0.9.6
113. Do. Do.	0.7.6
114. 3 small casks	0.9.0
115. Kneading trow	0.1.8
116. Safe, hoop & sieve	0.4.0
117. Sett of fire irons	0.6.6
	£100.18.0
Total amount of disbursements	72. 0.5
	£28.17.7

Augst 11th.1819 Settled Charles Courtenay

Disbursements

Paid for the carriage of the Catalogues	0.1.4
Paid Cryer	0.2.0
Paid Jenkins as per bill	1.8.7
Paid Dav. Jenkins	0.3.6
Duty	5.1.0
Making a catalogue, selling, collecting.the money &c.	4.4.0
Cash advanced	61.0.0
	£72.0.5

Glossary and Notes

7. Iron footman. A four-legged trivet of wrought iron with a flat top, used as a muffin or kettle stand. The top was level with a fire in a grate. Also used to keep plates hot (Gloag). In the Old Hall 1762 inventory there was an iron footman in the kitchen. For other references, see under 83 (plate warmer).

10. Iron digester. A stock-pot, for boiling down bones, etc. (OED).

12. Bell mettle. Bell metal, a tin, copper and zinc alloy resembling bronze.

15. Japan. Japanning, a kind of painting (Sheraton). Most frequently black and in general derived from the Japanese painting, as opposed to lacquering, fashionable from the late 17th century onwards.

21. Knife tray. Mahogany knife trays of the best kind have two partitions, with a brass handle which clasps over the edges of two

partitions, and screws to the sides, which are 3 or 3½ inches deep; the inside length 14 inches, and the width from 10 to 12 inches; observe, the sides of these knife trays are square up, not sloped as formerly (Sheraton).

22. Japan waiters. Presumably, at only 6d, small painted metal trays or salvers (OED). In the Old Hall 1762 inventory there were '3 small mahogany waiters' in the kitchen, and in the 1778 sale there were 'a large waiter' and 'two small ditto' in the butler's pantry. Also, in 1762 under 'plate', a 'Pontypool tea board' (a metal tray with japanned decoration made at Pontypool) and a waiter do. Mrs Margaret Gamage had a small waiter in the kitchen and another under 'silver plate' (Cilybebyll inventory, 1778)

    An intriguing item in the Old Hall 1762 inventory is '7 mohogany stands to hold dishes on the table' in the hall. These would appear to be self-service things, perhaps for dessert, enabling the room to be early vacated by the servants (very necessary when business talk and gossip were the rule!)

28, 29. Green chairs. Very likely to have been Windsor chairs. Green painted examples were popular in gentry houses for casual use, often out of doors.

33. Pier looking glass. A tall looking glass, occupying a pier between windows.

38. Mahy. Celeret. A small mahogany chest probably with sloped sides, having an inner lining divided into six or more partitions to hold wine bottles. An item of dining-room furniture. Many sideboards had a 'celeret drawer' for this purpose.

45. Eight day clock. A long-case movement running eight days before winding. Simpler, cheaper movements were wound every 24 hours, and very superior ones might be month-going or even longer. From its value at 7 guineas, it is quite likely to have been a Henry Williams of Llancarfan piece.

46. Clothes flasks. Clothes baskets (OED).

47. Beech tent bedstead. A folding bed-frame of beech wood, with a removable canopied tester etc. Tent or camp beds were in general use in bedrooms during the first half of the 19th century. Their attractive 'snug yet genteel look' (Boswell, 1762) gave them an appeal beyond their original purpose. They were extensively used for travelling, to avoid verminous beds in inns.

53. Deal dressing table. Dressing-tables in smart bedrooms were often of deal (pine) because they were entirely covered with a fine cloth, usually white, called a 'toilet'.
54. Fancy chairs. Lightweight, ornamented chairs, probably cane-seated or upholstered.
56. Bed w[eigh]t etc. The 'bed' refers in general to the movable mattresses, feather bedding if used, and the bolsters and pillows (Sheraton). Unusually, there is no reference in this inventory to the materials used (e.g. hair, flock) but it was usual for the better class of bedding to have two or more mattresses. The practice of selling by weight is so far unknown elsewhere and may simply be the local auctioneer's convenient way of putting it together in lots. The different prices per pound (1/6d, 1/7d and 1/10d) must reflect varying quality.
68. Bedstead & furniture. The bed framing and attached upholstery, as curtains, tester, valance etc., as opposed to the separate bedding laid on it.
81. Wooden clock. A rare reference at this time. British movements, with wheels cut in hard close-grained woods such as box, were known in the 18th century, but the majority found are later 19th century items imported from the Black Forest region of Germany. The low value of 8/- probably indicates a cheap foreign import even at this date. Wooden clocks were made as early as the late 17th century in Britain and, at least fifty years earlier than this example, in Germany (information from Michael Legg). Furthermore, wooden clocks were brought into Britain by itinerant clock sellers from Germany as early as 1800 (information from William Linnard). So it is likely that this was a German clock.
82. Toasting screen. Probably a vertical open rack to hold toast in front of the fire, possibly supported on a metal stand, like a roaster or Dutch oven. Possibly a local auctioneer's term, describing what he saw. In the Old Hall 1762 inventory there is '1 brass toaster' and '4 steel ditto' in the kitchen.
83. Plate warmer. A device which stood before a fire, holding plates to be warmed or kept warm. There were various types, a common one being a 'cat', six turned spindles projecting from a turned ball centre. Which ever way you put it down it stood on its feet (hence the name) and the three uppermost spindles supported the plates.

In the Old Hall 1778 sale there was an 'Iron cat' in the great parlour, perhaps used there to warm plates before the 'Bath stove' in that room. Also in Old Hall in 1762 there were 'two twig plate warmers' in the kitchen, probably open wickerwork baskets, one later described by the auctioneer in 1778 as 'a basket to warm plates before the fire', as well as a separate 'wicker plate basket', a 'copper plate warmer' and a 'footman'.

85. Dinner tray. The dinner tray is for taking up dishes and plates to the dining table; their sides are 3½" deep all round, with handle holes in each side which may be made of good Honduras [mahogany], but the bottoms should be of Spanish. The length of the largest dinner trays are 32", and width 2 feet; full size tea trays are nearly the same (Sheraton). In the Old Hall 1778 sale there were 'One mahogany dinner tray' and 'one ditto glass ditto' and 'one ditto small ditto'.

88. Plate basket. A china plate basket. Such baskets, made of mahogany, with fretwork sides and a brass hooped handle, were used for carrying heated plates from the kitchen to the dining-room, where they could be transferred to the haster (aka a plate warmer or a footman) set down by the fire to keep them warm. The basket had an octagonal base and seven vertical panels or facets, the eighth being omitted to allow the plates to be piled and lifted out easily (Gloag).

92. Coat jack. Possibly one of the uses of this term as a lifting or holding device, i.e. a coat stand or hanger.

93. Stable bucket & 2 pails. The terms bucket and pail were apparently synonymous.

100. Vat. A vessel, probably wooden, for brewing the malt (mashing) and, after boiling and cooling, to contain the fermenting wort. This use of a dual purpose vessel indicates a modest, farmhouse scale production, probably making both strong ale and 'small beer' (OED).

101. Cooler. A shallow vessel, having a large surface area, for cooling the hot wort after boiling with hops and before fermenting it.

103. Funnel, mashing stick and cross stick. Brewing equipment. The funnel was probably for delivering the loose hops. The mashing stick was probably a stick with other short sticks fixed through it to make a stirrer to stir the hot mash. The cross stick was probably

a split stick which, laid across the mash tub, provided a springgrip to hold the wort stick as it was gradually raised to allow the wort to run out. See William Cobbett, *Cottage Economy* (1831). Old Hall had a brewhouse where we find in 1762 '3 brewing vates', '2 trandells' (unidentified) and two 'brass boylers', together with pails etc.

115. Kneading trow. A trough for kneading dough.

A Note on Llanblethian Cottage by the Editor

The view of Llanblethian Cottage in a mid-nineteenth-century watercolour by Col. W. H. Taynton indicates that it was a substantial Georgian house with a veranda, not unlike the neighbouring Hill House. Edward Sterling and his family lived there from 1809 to 1814 and they were succeeded by Charles Courtenay who was almost certainly, by a change of name, later to become Sir Charles Throckmorton, the seventh baronet of Coughton Court, Warwickshire. The old house was demolished at the very end of the nineteenth century and the Vicarage (now the Old Vicarage) was built on the site.

Watercolour by Col. W. H. Taynton, c.1850. *Cowbridge History Society.*

SOURCES

The Courtenay inventory is in the Warwickshire County Record Office, CR 1998 Box 83.

The two Old Hall documents are in the Glamorgan Archives, the 1762 inventory is DEd 450, the printed sale catalogue of 1778 is DE 689.

Margaret Gamage's inventory is in the National Library of Wales, Cilybebyll 247.

Alden, Jeff (ed.), *Llanblethian: Buildings and People* (Cowbridge Record Society, 2001).

Cloutman, E. W. & Linnard, W., *Henry Williams Lancarvan: 'a Clock and Watchmaker. . .' in the Vale of Glamorgan* (Cardiff, 2003).

Gloag, John, *A Short Dictionary of Furniture* (London, 1969).

Oxford English Dictionary.

Sheraton, Thomas, *The Cabinet Dictionary* (London, 1803).

Thomas, Hilary M.(ed.), *Historic Gardens of the Vale of Glamorgan* (Welsh Historic Gardens Trust, South and Mid Glamorgan Branch, 2007).

THE ORIGINS OF RAMOTH CHAPEL, COWBRIDGE

By Brian James

Ramoth goes back to 1806, just over two hundred years ago; it was then a Welsh Baptist congregation. But the story really begins three hundred years ago - in the early part of the eighteenth century. At that time there were two Baptist churches in Glamorgan, the one in the west at Swansea, the other in the east at Hengoed in the Rhymney Valley. The members were few and they lived all over the county, mostly in the Uplands. Their dwellings were scattered and only in the summer months could they assemble in either of the chapels, given the difficulties of travel in those days. There were teams of ministers who went out to private houses across the county to hold Sunday services and to administer the monthly communion.

As numbers slowly increased, it became possible to think of an additional chapel; this was built in 1718 at Pen-y-fai, a mile or so north of Bridgend, conveniently situated roughly half way between Swansea and Hengoed. To Pen-y-fai can be traced all the Baptist congregations in the central part of Glamorgan, as far east as Cowbridge and as far west as Port Talbot.

There is no need to go into detail about how the Baptists spread across mid-Glamorgan. I'll just mention Nottage and Wick, which began as branches of Pen-y-fai. From Wick a congregation was established at Ewenny around 1800. A few years later the Ewenny Baptists built a chapel at the top of Newcastle Hill, Bridgend - it was given the name Ruhamah, after an obscure character in the Book of Hosea. Ruhamah is the mother church of Ramoth, Cowbridge.

At the beginning of 1806 a group of people from Ruhamah registered in the Bishop of Llandaff's court what they described as 'a house called Ramoth lately in the tenure and occupation of Mr Hunt', in Cowbridge. They were obliged by law to inform the Bishop that they were starting a new meeting house. This building was actually a former malthouse behind number 31 High Street (the Delicatessen shop at the present time, then a baker's belonging to Thomas Hunt). The old malthouse and the first Ramoth is still there.

These were very bold moves on the part of Ruhamah: to send preachers to Cowbridge and then to rent a place for their converts to meet, for Cowbridge was a stronghold of the Church of England, then the Established Church. Everyone who was anyone in Cowbridge would have attended the parish church. Furthermore, the Grammar School, presided over by the eminent churchman, the Rev. Dr William Williams, exercised a strong Anglican influence in the town and neighbourhood; attached to the Grammar School was a divinity school in which young men were prepared for ordination.

Why did the Baptists choose the name Ramoth? It is a rare name for a chapel - there seem to be only four others in the whole of Wales, where there are thousands of chapels. Since all four are Baptist chapels, it is possible that they were all named after the one in Merioneth, where there was a very well known Baptist preacher at the time: 'J. R. Jones, Ramoth' as he was called. That is just a possibility. The original Ramoth was a city in Gilead, mentioned in the Book of Deuteronomy.

The first Baptists to venture into Cowbridge were not likely to have found a welcome among the elite of the town. Very little is actually known about who the first converts were, except for one Richard Rees. He was described in his obituary notice in the local press in 1846 as 'the first who joined the Baptist connexion at Cowbridge 40 years ago'. He was a stonemason by trade and there will be more to say about him shortly.

The Baptists continued to meet in the old malthouse for about twelve years. Meanwhile membership was growing and they began to look around for a site to build their own chapel. One of the Ruhamah ministers came to live in Cowbridge in 1816-17 - presumably in an effort to strengthen the congregation. They were able to move to their second Ramoth in 1818.

How this became possible very much involved Richard Rees already mentioned as the first Baptist convert in Cowbridge. If there are heroes in this story then Richard Rees is one of them. He was a stonemason, but became what nowadays would be called a builder, even a property developer. In 1812 he bought a piece of ground on Westgate, fronted by an old cottage and a barn, with a long garden behind - to those who know the history of medieval Cowbridge this was a double 'burgage plot' which rendered two shillings a year to the Marquess of Bute, the lord of the borough of Cowbridge. The vendor was the Dunraven Estate and Rees paid £100 for the property. It seems that he redeveloped the street frontage as two cottages, now numbers 21 and 23 Westgate; the long garden at the back became the site of Ramoth.

Nobody knows what Ramoth II was like - it would not be unreasonable to assume that it was smaller, plainer and more cheaply built than the present chapel, Ramoth III. There is every reason to suppose that it was built by the firm of Richard Rees - who else? When the building was registered with the Bishop of Llandaff as a place of nonconformist worship in July 1818, two of the signatories were Richard Rees and the other hero of this story: John Roberts of Sigginston.

Although they now had their own brand-new chapel, the people of Ramoth were still technically members of Ruhamah, Bridgend. The next step was obviously to take over responsibility for their own affairs by becoming a separate Baptist church and appointing their own minister and officers. This was done in 1820 and John Roberts was chosen and ordained as minister. (A report appeared in the Welsh magazine, *Seren Gomer*, III, 1820, p. 187.) He was a very remarkable man.

From the affectionate account of Roberts written by his friend, the minister of Ruhamah, and from his own all-too-brief autobiography, we learn a good deal about his life and character.

He was born in 1787 at Llanmaes, the son of a labourer. The family moved a few years later to Llansannor, where John grew up and where he had his first job working on the Llansannor Estate owned by J. F. Gwyn, but not before he had had a short period of formal education, aged ten, at the Eagle Academy in Cowbridge. His father could not afford to give him more.

In 1804 John Roberts was apprenticed to a blacksmith in Cowbridge. After serving his time he married and took a job in Neath. It was there that he was baptised (or rather, rebaptised since he had been baptised by the curate of Llanmaes as an infant), became a member of a Baptist church and began to preach. In 1809 he moved back to the Cowbridge area and set up his own smithy at Sigginston. That provided his livelihood for most of the rest of his life - for although Ramoth ordained him, they were never able to pay him a living wage.

As a preacher, John Roberts was successful and popular. Despite his having had only a brief period of schooling, he became a great reader and student, with a remarkably retentive memory for what he had read. His biographer refers to his eloquence, his loving manner, his sweet voice and his humble bearing. As a preacher he was no hot gospeller nor a hell-fire-

Ramoth Chapel, Photograph 1981. *Cowbridge History Society.*

damnation man, as so many of his contemporaries were. His preaching was not directed to the conversion of his congregation but towards expounding to them the promises of the gospel, the love of God and, above all, divine providence. In Roberts's autobiography the word 'Rhagluniaeth' stands out - that is the Welsh word for providence. He saw God's providence in every turning-point of his life.

Roberts was loved by the people of Ramoth and respected by the neighbourhood in general. He was clearly something of a saint.

Ramoth was thriving as a church in the 1820s. John Roberts tells us that he baptised 209 persons during his fifteen years' ministry at Cowbridge, that is from 1820 to 1835. A larger chapel would soon be necessary to accommodate the growing congregation. This would be the third Ramoth, dating from 1828-29 - the chapel which still stands, not having been altered much in the last 186 years.

We are told by an historian of the Baptist denomination (David Jones of Carmarthen), writing ten years later, that the new building had cost £1,200. It is difficult to make comparisons, but there is no doubt that that was a large amount; most chapels built in the 1820s cost *far* less. (For example, the Baptist chapel at Llancarfan was built for £358 in 1823.) This expenditure was certainly too much for the congregation - they could not afford it, and at the time of John Roberts's death in 1835 there was an unpaid debt on the building of £700, that is to say, more than half the amount was still outstanding.

The result was, of course, an exceptionally fine chapel. John Newman, the scholarly author of the Glamorgan volume in the Pevsner series (1995), calls Ramoth 'one of the best early chapels in the county'. The building, even though it is largely hidden from the view of casual visitors, is undoubtedly one of the gems of Cowbridge. Why did the local Baptists, led by John Roberts and Richard Rees, risk financial disaster to build it? Of course, they had faith that the Lord would provide. An interesting account of their motives is given by the Baptist historian just mentioned. This is what he said (in translation):

> The faithful minister was thinking that the wealthy inhabitants of the town would come to a splendid meeting house more than they did [before]; but the truth is that a large debt on a chapel is an obstacle to wealthy people coming to it, because they think that it would oblige them to take a share in the burden; and so it has happened in this place. (David Jones, *Hanes y Bedyddwyr yn Neheubarth Cymru,* p. 620.)

So John Roberts wanted to raise the standing of the Baptist cause amongst the townspeople of Cowbridge.

It would be interesting to know who designed Ramoth III. There is a hint of architecture about it, where older chapels in South Wales had been simple cottage-like or barn-like structures - some of them had actually been cottages or barns adapted as places of worship. The first chapel at Aberthin is an example. But there is no reason to think that a professional architect was actually employed. The likelihood is that John Roberts and Richard Rees between them had designed the building.

Something that writers on local buildings don't seem to have noticed is that there is another chapel almost identical to Ramoth: this is Bethel, the

Baptist chapel in Llantwit Major, which dates from 1830. It would be interesting to know if John Roberts and Richard Rees were responsible for that too.

John Newman is enthusiastic about Ramoth, as mentioned before. He illustrates it with two photographs (interior and exterior), but he is not entirely accurate in his description of the building. He refers to its 'pyramid' roof - it does seem to be so if you stand in front, but move to the side (along Broadshoard) and it is obvious that the roof is not pyramidal at all: it is what architects call 'hipped'. Newman also refers to the 'square interior' - but if the building is not quite square, it is certainly squarish.

The people of Ramoth did not mark the opening of their splendid new chapel in the usual way. What they did was to invite the Association of Baptists of South-east Wales (Cymanfa Dde-ddwyreiniol y Bedyddwyr) to hold their annual assembly in Cowbridge; that was in June 1829. The meeting extended over three days and large congregations listened to an extravaganza of eleven sermons preached by some of the stars of the Welsh pulpit; the best known of them was Christmas Evans, at that time minister of the Tabernacle in Cardiff. An evening service on the first day was held in a field, presumably because there were too many hearers for the seating capacity of the chapel. (A report appeared in *Greal y Bedyddwyr*, III, 1829, p. 220.)

The 1830s were a difficult time for the church at Ramoth. The unpaid debt on the chapel was a serious burden. The church asked John Roberts to give up his trade and to move from Sigginston into town. He could then devote his whole time to the ministry, but they were not able to pay him a living wage and he was obliged to go to preach to the Baptists of Caerphilly two Sundays in the month. He also undertook long and exhausting preaching tours - this was the approved method of collecting money towards paying off chapel debt. The minister would preach wherever he could get a hearing and afterwards a collection would be taken up.

John Roberts's biographer expressed the opinion that all this travelling damaged his health. In fact, his health broke down after his return from a tour in England in 1834. He had to give up the Sunday visits to Caerphilly and he was never well again. He died of cancer in April 1835, aged forty-eight.

It was thought that about 2,000 people of every rank and religious denomination came to his funeral at Ramoth, showing how universally regarded he was. Of course the chapel could not accommodate such a number. It is likely that the vague estimate included the people who stood in the graveyard and even those who lined the street outside to pay their respects.

Forward now to the 1840s, a time when prosperity returned to Ramoth. A succession of three ministers transformed the situation. They did not stay long in Cowbridge - it was just another place which they passed through in their long ministerial careers. They could not have been more different from John Roberts: they were not local men, they were better educated, they were professional preachers and prominent in the denomination; they published books and articles; they preached in a much more aggressive way than the gentle blacksmith. In fact, they were loud, hot gospellers whose aim was the conversion of those who listened to them. This type of ministry seems to have been what the public wanted. Membership at Ramoth increased from eighty in 1839 to 156 in 1846, while the entire congregation, made up of members and non-members and, of course, children, was much larger than that. The usual practice in Welsh chapels was for non-members (known as 'adherents or hearers') to sit in the gallery - so preachers would direct their stirring message 'to the gallery' with the object of bringing them into membership. Ramoth seems to have been full for a normal Sunday evening service.

The first of the three ministers, Thomas Morris, was a native of Carmarthenshire. He arrived in Cowbridge in 1840 and left in 1842. What he achieved in only two years is almost incredible. According to his grandson, E. W. Miles, he cleared the remaining debt, he renovated the chapel, and he baptised more than sixty converts in his first year. (It is interesting to note that the custom was to baptise in the River Thaw in the summer months and in the chapel - where there was a baptistery or baptism pool - at other times of the year.)

So famous was Thomas Morris among the Baptists of South Wales that he was nicknamed 'Twm Deg Capel' (Ten Chapel Tom) on account of his having built or enlarged ten chapels in the course of his career. Ramoth was apparently one of the ten, but what he actually did to the building, which was only twelve years old, is not at all clear - did he merely have it redecorated? There seems to be no record, but it is possible that the schoolroom was added to the side of the chapel in his time.

Thomas Morris moved on to Corntown and Pyle and was succeeded at Ramoth by Daniel Jones, another Carmarthenshire man. His entry in the

Dictionary of Welsh Biography describes him as one of the greatest preachers of his denomination. The most significant event at Ramoth in his time was the founding of a branch chapel at Colwinston. It cost only £70, which suggests that it was adapted from an existing building and that materials and labour were provided free. (A report in *Y Bedyddiwr*, II, 1843, p. 284.)

The climax of this story comes in March 1851. The third of the new generation of ministers, John Evans, from Llanidloes in Montgomeryshire, was faced with the unique problem of filling in a special census form; that year the Government had decided to conduct a 'religious census'. No one at that time was used to filling in forms, and nonconformist ministers were not at ease with figures and statistics - some, indeed, had a theological objection to numbering the people. John Evans stated that the average attendance at morning service was 150 to 200 and at evening service 500. Very round figures, but they are quite believable. But seriously over-the-top was his comment 'I have seen a thousand in the chapel in the evening before now'. Since he had just written on the census form that the chapel had space for 480, with additional standing room for 200, we must accept that 1,000 is a bit of an exaggeration.

Nevertheless, there is no doubt that Ramoth was in a flourishing state in the middle years of the nineteenth century; its congregation was the largest belonging to any of the five places of worship within the borough of Cowbridge, though the Limes Chapel (which was Calvinistic Methodist) was a close second.

An aspect of this prosperity is rather unexpected, not to say surprising. Ramoth became the most popular venue in Cowbridge for weddings.

Before 1837 Anglican churches had a monopoly on marriages. From that year it became legal to marry in nonconformist chapels provided that they had been licensed by the Registrar General. Ramoth was so licensed in 1841 and the first wedding there was that of the minister's daughter, Mary Ann Morris, who married Thomas Miles who had a grocer's shop in Cowbridge High Street.

There were not many weddings in the first few years, but around 1850 there were nine or ten in a year, and the minister was claiming that more people were getting married in Ramoth than in Holy Cross Church (then known as St Mary's). There had been at least seventy-two marriages in the chapel by 1855. From the very sketchy information that is to hand, it seems that the couples came not just from Cowbridge itself but from country districts for miles around. The reason for that was that as yet very few local chapels had been licensed for marriages. Ramoth's main rival in that respect was Saron, the Independent chapel at Treoes.

Well, with the 1850s I have reached the end of what I have to say about the history of the founding of Ramoth. There are 160 more years yet to come, and I very much hope that someone else will carry the story forward to the present day.

SOURCES

'Bywgraffiad y Parch. John Roberts', *Greal y Bedyddwyr*, IX (1835), 321-4.

Jones, Anthony, *Welsh Chapels* (Stroud, 1996).

Jones, David, *Hanes y Bedyddwyr yn Neheubarth Cymru* (Carmarthen, 1839).

Jones, Ieuan Gwynedd & Williams. David (eds.), *The Religious Census of 1851,* Vol. I, *South Wales* (Cardiff, 1976).

Newman, John, *Glamorgan* (London & Cardiff, 1995).

Richards, John, *The Cowbridge Story* (Bridgend, 1956).

A HISTORY OF COWBRIDGE POLICE

By Nicole Burnett

At the time this article was written [1998] I had the dual roles of Curator of the South Wales Police Museum and Development Officer for the Cowbridge and District Museum. I decided then to combine the two and to write a history of policing in Cowbridge.

How the Police Began

Sir Robert Peel established the Metropolitan Police - the first professional police force - in 1829. Cowbridge fell within the catchment area of the Glamorgan Constabulary which was formed in 1841, the first county police force in Wales. The magistrates meeting in quarter sessions were responsible for the government of the county, and in 1839 the County Police Act was passed by Parliament giving them the power to establish a police force paid for by the general county rate. For years the magistrates fought against the idea of a county-wide force since they felt that the less affluent rural areas of the county would unfairly have to pay for the policing of the rapidly expanding industrial areas. It was also felt that rural communities had no need of a police force and that the time-honoured system of annually-elected parish constables was sufficient.

At this time Cowbridge, a small town in a thriving agricultural area, was served by six parish constables. These men were both unpaid and untrained. Each was given a truncheon and a stave as 'staffs of office', which acted very much like the warrant cards of today. These truncheons and staves can be seen on display in the Council Chamber of Cowbridge Town Hall.

On the 29 June 1841, after much persuasion by the second Marquess of Bute, the magistrates in quarter sessions resolved:

> It has been made to appear that the ordinary officers appointed for preserving the peace within this County are not sufficient for the preservation of the peace and for the protection of the inhabitants and for security of property within this County.

Therefore the Glamorgan Constabulary was formed. The new force comprised one chief constable, Captain Charles Frederick Napier, one superintendent for each of four divisions of the county, and thirty-four constables.

Sergeant Thomas Thomas

Cowbridge belonged to the Ogmore division and was initially policed by just one constable, thought to have been a P. C. Stephen Adams. In 1853 he was replaced by Sergeant Thomas Thomas, who remained the Cowbridge policeman until 1868. Sergeant Thomas was a native of the Neath area and had been stationed at Pyle, Aberkenfig and Llantwit Major before being posted to Cowbridge. A description of Sergeant Thomas was written by E. W. Miles who was born in Cowbridge in 1852:

Sergeant Thomas Thomas, the Cowbridge policeman from 1853 to 1868. This is an early kind of photograph called an 'ambrotype', a positive image on glass. *Glamorgan Archives.*

> There was only one police officer here then, but on fair days a few more were imported. The officer, Sergeant Thomas, was a man of fine physique, wore a dark uniform and a tall glazed hat, generally known as a box hat. The police station was then at the base of the Town Hall on the western side, and the justices' court was in the ante-room of the Hall, now the platform. . . This Sergeant Thomas was friendly with my father, and when I was a child had the privilege of inspecting the cells with him, when the Sergeant as a joke closed the ponderous door and left me alone in practically total darkness. It was a severe shock although only for a few seconds or so, and it created a lifelong conception of solitary confinement.

Cowbridge Police Stations

The cells were remnants from the days of the House of Correction or Bridewell, over which the Town Hall was built in 1830. Even in Victorian times they were thought to be outdated and inappropriate for police use, as can be seen from the chief constable's report dated 31 March 1859:

> For some years the constable stationed at Cowbridge has been permitted to use the cells under the old Town Hall for police purposes. They are very damp and badly ventilated and without the usual convenience generally supplied to cells. After heavy falls of rain there is ½ inch or more of water on the floor and of course at these times the cells are unavailable. I consider them as quite unfit for the temporary confinement of prisoners.

At the Easter quarter sessions of 1859 the problem was discussed and it was resolved 'That a police station with cells and accommodation for two constables be erected at Cowbridge'.

By Michaelmas 1860 a parcel of land had been leased from the Rev. Thomas Edmondes of Old Hall for £8 per annum for a police station. Finally, in the November of 1862, Cowbridge's new police station was opened, with three cells and accommodation for two constables. Sergeant Thomas was the first officer to be stationed there, and he remained until he left the town on his promotion to inspector in 1868.

The Police Station, c.1900. *Cowbridge History Society.*

SOURCES

Information for this article was taken from the extensive South Wales Police archives held at the Glamorgan Record Office (now the Glamorgan Archives) in Cardiff.

FURTHER READING

Baker, E. R., 'The beginnings of the Glamorgan County Police', *Glamorgan Historian*, Vol. 2 (1965), pp. 40-52.

Richards, John, *The Cowbridge Story* (Bridgend, 1956), pp. 73-6.

BRUNEL, THE SOUTH WALES RAILWAY AND COWBRIDGE

By Don Gerrard

Isambard Kingdom Brunel (1806-59) was an engineer of outstanding originality, arguably the finest ever produced by Britain. He was the son of a French emigré, Sir Marc Brunel, himself a famous engineer who had solved the problem of underwater tunnelling. The younger Brunel was appointed Resident Engineer of the Thames Tunnel in 1825, and in 1830 his design for the Clifton Suspension Bridge was accepted in preference to that submitted by Thomas Telford. He also designed docks at Bristol, Brentford, Briton Ferry, Milford Haven and Plymouth, and three famous steamships - the *Great Western,* the *Great Britain*, and the *Great Eastern.*

It was however as a railway engineer that he is best known. In 1833 he became chief engineer of the Great Western Railway, and the London to Bristol line was probably the finest main line built anywhere in the Railway Age, with its gentle curves and slight gradients, the famous Box Tunnel and the terminus at Temple Meads. He introduced the broad gauge (7ft 0¼"), as opposed to Stephenson's 4ft 8½ inches, which made high speeds possible. He designed and built over 1,000 miles of railways in the West Country, South Wales and the Midlands. It was Brunel's plans for the extension of the GWR from Bristol into South Wales (the South Wales Railway) that had a great impact on Cowbridge.

Cowbridge was probably at the peak of its prosperity in the first half of the nineteenth century. The road through the town was made a turnpike road in 1764, and by 1786 there was a regular mail coach service using the *Bear Hotel* as an intermediary stop. There were two attempts to build a tramway to Cowbridge (similar to that from Maesteg to Bridgend and Porthcawl) in 1816 from Llanharry colliery, and in 1825 from Trecastle colliery, near Pontyclun. In 1825 there was a meeting at the *Bear Hotel* to promote such a tramway, with an extension to Aberthaw. However, nothing came of it.

In 1844 the South Wales Railway was proposed, and sanctioned by Act of Parliament in 1845 as a broad gauge line. Work began in 1846 and the route from Gloucester to Cardiff, Bridgend, Neath and Swansea was surveyed personally by Brunel. It appeared to Brunel that by far the best and shortest route would be across the Vale of Glamorgan via Cowbridge, a prospect that did not meet with the approval of the Corporation or the inhabitants. Whether this influenced the choice of route is not known. It has been suggested that there would have been engineering difficulties in crossing the Thaw Valley, although these would not have been as great as those experienced by Brunel at Landore and Llansamlet. The 1844 prospectus for the railway stated that 'from Cardiff the railway passes through the rich agricultural district adjacent to. . . Cowbridge, Bridgend, Porthcawl and Pyle', and later 'the proposed railroad will run through the coal works about 5 miles to the north of Cowbridge, and the good people of the ancient borough are well pleased to be left undisturbed'. Because of this it was suggested that 'Cowbridge is an old-fashioned town, consisting of one long street, which is likely to bear a crop of grass as soon as the South Wales Railway is in operation' (C. F. Cliffe).

Not all the inhabitants of Cowbridge were hostile to the railway. The Rev. Thomas Edmondes, the Vicar of Cowbridge, ran a concerted campaign to have the railway run through the town, although he later became convinced that the route via Pontyclun was chosen for engineering reasons. David Jones of Wallington said 'No one had ever believed the action of the Corporation to have compelled the South Wales Railway to pass by Cowbridge. . . they were hostile to the railway when as guardians of the welfare of the town, they should have taken active steps in getting the railway to enter their neighbourhood' (quoted by C. Chapman).

The line from Cardiff to Swansea opened on 18 June 1850. The effect on South Wales was immediate. It was no longer remote, the growth of the coal industry was accelerated - in 1845 there were seven pits in the Aberdare valley, by 1855 there were twenty-eight. The Taff Vale Railway was engineered by Brunel, so that twenty new pits were opened in the Rhondda Valley between 1865 and 1875. Before this the Rhondda was a 'wild, untouched, mountainous region, where the lark sang and a Sabbath sweetness reigned' (F. Booker). It was never to be the same again: 'its pastoral stillness was shattered forever' (F. Booker). The first trainload of coal reached Cardiff in 1855, and soon Rhondda coal, the finest steam coal in the world, fuelled the Navy and the world's merchant ships.

There was great excitement in Cardiff on the opening day of the South Wales Railway. Its construction had brought about a major change in the face of the town: the course of the Taff had been altered enabling Westgate Street to be built and Cardiff Arms Park to be created. Local dignitaries met the first train, hordes of people were at the station, some even on the roof. At Bridgend a band paraded through the streets four hours before the train was due to arrive, and hundreds of people were on the streets and at the station. 'This attitude contrasted with that of the people of Cowbridge, who decided that they did not want. . . the railway. . . anywhere near them, and lived to regret it as trade slumped with the extinction of stage coach travel' (H. Williams). At every stop along the line to Swansea there were huge crowds, the pealing of church bells and the flying of flags. (The journey from Cardiff to Bridgend took one hour, the second-class fare was 1/6d. From Bridgend to London cost 15/6d.)

The effect on Cowbridge too was immediate. The mail coach service was withdrawn a month later, in July 1850. The Quarter Sessions were held for the last time in Cowbridge in 1850, and the town soon began to stagnate. The *Cardiff and Merthyr Guardian* suggested in 1853 that 'the want of a railway reduces Cowbridge. . . to a state of hopeless isolation. . . and confines Cowbridge to the humble position of a small country market town'.

There began almost immediately agitation in the town for the construction of a railway, a branch from Llantrisant or a loop line from Peterston-super-Ely through Cowbridge to Bridgend. Five long years of agitation followed. In December 1855 a public meeting was held at the Town Hall, and a committee was formed to press for a branch line from Llantrisant to Cowbridge. This ended in failure, and another meeting at the Town Hall in September 1860 with the mayor, R. C. Nicholl Carne, in the chair, recommended the building of an independent railway from Cowbridge to Llantrisant at an estimated cost of £25,000. A further meeting in October 1860 suggested the railway be built by the Taff Vale Railway Company, but the project came to nothing.

Finally, in 1861 a committee was formed to promote the Cowbridge Railway! A prospectus was issued with a capital of £30,000, and the Taff Vale Railway agreed to subscribe £5,000. There was however great difficulty in raising funds in Cowbridge. 'Tradespeople came forward with modest sums, but the wealthy landowners seemed reluctant to support the venture' (C. Chapman).

Despite the shortfall in capital, plans went ahead and in June 1862 the Cowbridge Railway Bill was passed. There were great celebrations in the town, and the GWR agreed to assist with costs (the South Wales Railway sold out to the GWR in 1863) despite continuing difficulties in raising funds. In April 1863 Messrs. Griffiths and Thomas were appointed contractors, the engineer being Alexander Bassett, a man who belonged to a prominent local family. On 9 June Dr J. W. Nicholl Carne cut the first sod. The town was packed, there was a procession headed by a band to the proposed terminus in Eastgate, and a public dinner was held at the *Bear Hotel* that evening. Although construction work on the railway was slow, largely due to men being taken away during harvesting, the railway was completed on 12 December 1864. The Cowbridge Railway was ready to start operating.

SOURCES AND FURTHER READING

Booker, Frank, *The Great Western Railway* (Atlantic Transport Publications, 1985).
Cliffe, C. F., *The Book of South Wales* (London, 1847; reprinted Nabu Press, 2013).
Chapman, Colin, *The Cowbridge Railway* (Poole, Oxford Publishing Co., 1984).
Williams, Herbert, *Railways in Wales* (Swansea, Christopher Davies, 1977).
Cardiff and Merthyr Guardian.
Glamorgan Gazette.

COWBRIDGE AND THE BLUE BOOKS

By Nigel Williams

In 1846 William Williams, M.P. for Coventry, convinced the government of the time of the need to launch a commission of inquiry into the provision of education in Wales. The inquiry was conducted by three English barristers with eight assistants, seven of whom were Anglicans. Their report, published in 1847, and commonly called the Blue Books after the colour of the cover, caused a furore, and can still raise blood pressure in some people today. How did Cowbridge fare from the visit of David Lewis, a student at Lampeter and one of the eight assistant commissioners?

Lewis seemingly was not expecting to visit the Grammar School, for the Commission was only required to consider education provision within the means of the poorer classes. However, he was assailed by John Bevan, the Cowbridge solicitor, then living at Newton House, concerning the fixed money payments from Jesus College, Oxford, and the provision of free places under the will of Sir Leoline Jenkins. In one of the few attempts at objectivity in the report, the views of the headmaster were sought and both sides of the argument were presented without comment.

Lewis did not visit the Eagle Academy in Westgate, merely noting that it 'enjoys a very extensive reputation as a commercial school, but is beyond the reach of the poor'. In his evidence to the Commission, the Rev. Thomas Edmondes commented that the smaller farmers tended to send their children there.

Lewis visited the National School on Cardiff Road on 12 March 1847. (The building is now a private house, the last on the road leaving Cowbridge towards Cardiff.) The school had been established in 1839 and, though the building itself was in good condition, the outbuildings were deemed insufficient. The schoolroom measured 31 feet by 18 feet by 12 feet and, according to the formula used by the Commission, could accommodate ninety-three children. The equipment was insufficient but in good repair, a comment which appeared constantly in the report. There were sixty-eight on the register and the master had taken up his post within the previous twelve months, the school having been closed for the preceding six months. Two girls and four boys were under five, four girls and thirty-nine boys were aged five to ten, and two girls and seventeen boys were over ten. Six of the latter group acted as pupil teachers.

Lewis heard eighteen boys and four girls read the first chapter of Luke. However, the group failed to answer questions about Aaron and the sacraments and did not know the words 'translated' and 'translation'. 4292 was subtracted from 5621, and 94381 divided by 526 correctly.

The master reported that attendance was irregular and many did not come to school more than two days a week. The master was not named. However, he was thirty-eight and had trained at Westminster Central for six months. His salary of £40 p.a. was made up from subscriptions. Census and church records suggest that he was Edward Seccombe Hodges, born in Mevagissey in Cornwall, and who had taught in Hawkesbury, Gloucestershire, before moving to Cowbridge, for its was there that his two sons were born. The Hodges family lived in The Cross, Llanblethian, and Edward was left a widower when his wife, Hannah, died three days after giving birth to their fourth child in 1850.

On 3 March Lewis visited all the dame schools, the first one being that run by Mrs Burton. In the 1851 Census a Mary Barton, aged sixty-four, is recorded as a schoolmistress living in West Village, next door to the Eagle Academy. The school, established in 1835, was held in her home in a room 18 feet by 18 feet by 10 feet, sufficient accommodation for fifty-four. There were fifteen children on the register - two boys under five, three girls and five boys aged between five and ten, and five girls over ten. According to Lewis, the children were only taught reading and the girls a little sewing. However, he found the children were all very orderly in their behaviour. Evidently Mary Barton had taken up teaching in her widowhood and it provided an income of some £10 8s. p.a.

Miss Harris had established her school in 1840. Again according to the Census of 1851, Catherine Harris, aged forty-nine, lived in East Village, at 51 Eastgate. The room measured 9 by 12 by 8 and was sufficient for eighteen pupils though there were twenty-six pupils on the register, including one boy under five, ten girls and five boys aged between five and ten, and ten girls over ten. Only sixteen girls and six boys were present. Lewis reported that the dame 'seemed a superior person; her scholars were farmers, tradesmen and mechanics' children. There was only one labourer's child in the school, and this one of the better class. . . This school was, upon the whole, a nice one'. Miss Harris had become a teacher at thirty-three and had spent her time before that at home or working linen. Her income from school pence was about £30 p.a.

Lewis was dismissive of the third school he visited - Mrs James's school. 'It scarcely deserves the name of school. When I first entered the house the dame had gone to church to supply the place of her husband, who is sexton, and was at work elsewhere. The next time she was out when I entered, but came in with a baby in her arms. I only found present six very young children, five of whom were reading Vyse's Spelling Book; the other was in the alphabet. The mistress told me that it was entirely for the convenience of her own children that she kept the school; and as her attention to her family was becoming more needed, she was very shortly to give it up.' It did however provide an income of £10 4s. p.a.

The assistants were also deputed to visit Sunday schools. The one attached to the Church was run by Mrs Barton in her home, with the help of the ladies of the town. Some fifty-four children - seven boys and forty-seven girls all under fifteen - attended and all were in education during the week. They seemed able to answer Lewis's questions to his satisfaction, though they said the Lord's Prayer 'in a very careless manner'.

Ramoth's Sunday school was held in the vestry. There were nine teachers and some forty-five pupils - twenty-five under fifteen years old and the rest over fifteen. They were usually taught together through the medium of both Welsh and English. When Lewis entered he found 'the children and four teachers seated round the fire, and the place presented anything but the appearance of a school'. He heard them read part of Matthew's Gospel in Welsh but they were unable to answer any of his questions. He reported 'I have never met more thoroughly ignorant children; they actually knew nothing'.

The Sunday school at Sion Chapel in the Limes catered for some sixty children, equally divided between under and over fifteens. Girls and boys were taught separately for some two hours each Sunday through the medium of English and Welsh. Their religious knowledge seemed somewhat stronger than that of the pupils at Ramoth. However, Lewis noted, 'they did not seem to be under any discipline whatever, but did what they pleased, and when they pleased'.

David Lewis completed his task by visiting the Sunday school at Ebenezer, the Wesleyan Methodist Chapel (probably then at 4 High Street, where the Filco car-park is now), on 7 March. There were some fifty-one pupils on the register, most of whom were under fifteen. School lasted two hours and was conducted through the medium of both English and Welsh. He heard groups read from the Gospels in both languages and received satisfactory answers to his questions from the group using English.

What can be drawn from this investigation into the provision of education in Cowbridge? Probably not a great deal. Suffice it to say that it received a mauling similar to that of most towns in Wales. Country-wide it made Nonconformity increasingly reluctant to accept state aid for education and soured their relationships with the Anglican Church. Eventually it resulted in the establishment of the undenominational Board Schools following the Education Act of 1870. The Blue Books also had political repercussions, for the controversy they created helped to shake Calvinistic Methodism in particular out of its acceptance of the status quo and into an active interest in radical and reforming politics.

SOURCES AND FURTHER READING

The famous 'Blue Books' were published in three volumes in 1847 with the official title: *Reports of the Commissioners of Inquiry into the State of Education in Wales.* Cowbridge will be found in Vol. I, pp. 314-6.

A brief general account of the Blue Books controversy ('Brad y Llyfrau Gleision') is given in John Davies, *A History of Wales* (London, 1992), pp. 390-3.

THE MURDER IN THE STORM

By Don Gerrard

In 1885 a farmer and cattle dealer named David Thomas resided at Stallcourt Farm, Llanblethian. He was married, with four children, had spent some years in America and was often referred to as 'The Yankee' in the parts of South Wales where he was well known. He was well known and popular within the district and had a reputation for generosity.

On 30 October 1885, Mr Thomas left his home early in the morning and caught the train from Cowbridge to the market at Treorchy. There his business dealings earned him £60, including a sovereign which had a hole in it. Mr Thomas placed all this loose money in a canvas bag he was in the habit of carrying and then went on to have dinner in a tavern in the town, met many acquaintances and drank with most of them.

He returned to Cowbridge by train, getting there at about 8.30 p.m. He was under the influence of alcohol but still capable of attending to business, for he was known to have received some more money from a farmer in the town. This man walked with Mr Thomas to the *Duke of Wellington* where both were well known as regular customers.

An elderly man named Edward Roberts, 'Ned the Sawyer', was present in the taproom. He and his son David were well known in the district, but few people cared to have much to do with them. David Roberts in particular was a heavy, loutish-looking man with a sullen expression and a thick, dark moustache. However, he and his father were devoted to one another and quite inseparable. They lived alone in their small two-roomed cottage in Piccadilly, Llanblethian, within a quarter of a mile of Stallcourt Farm, David having returned there some three months earlier after seven years in the army. David Roberts joined his father at the inn shortly before Mr Thomas arrived. David did not have any money and his father, Edward, paid for the drinks. They were joined by a third man, John Thomas the baker, a nephew of the cattle dealer.

David Thomas reached the *Duke of Wellington* at 9 p.m. and joined the Roberts party, paying for the first round of drinks. He took the money from the canvas bag and boastfully said, 'I am willing to lend anyone here £20', and rattled the heavy bag upon the table. In the absence of any takers, Thomas put the bag away and invited the others to join him in a game of cards.

Two drawings, probably from a contemporary newspaper report, of Stallcourt, the deceased's farmhouse in Llanblethian, and the site of the murder. *Cowbridge History Society.*

Edward Roberts was too drunk to play and fell asleep on a settle in the corner of the room. He was however able to leave the public house at 11 p.m. with the others. The four of them were seen going off together down Church Street and along Town Mill Road, Thomas and his nephew in front and the two Robertses following behind. A gale had sprung up and the rain came down in torrents. At Town Mill it is presumed that, after an argument overheard by Mr Alexander of the Mill, Mr Thomas turned right following the footpath to the foot of Mount Ida; the other three may have turned left to go through the Three Fields to Llanblethian.

At 7 a.m. the following morning a man named Benjamin Williams made a shocking discovery whilst on his way to work. He came upon the body of a man at a point half way between the stile at Town Mill and Stallcourt Farm. The man had been savagely murdered. The head and face had been battered so as to render him unrecognisable. There were terrible wounds at the back of his head, two wounds in the front of his face, and one wound on the left side of his nose, penetrating to the bone of his skull. This last injury, inflicted with some blunt, heavy instrument, must have been instantly fatal. The rain had ceased about 2 a.m. but, as the dead man's clothes were saturated, it was clear that he had been attacked and killed before that hour. His pockets were turned out and no money was found on him. There was a notebook and one or two small articles, but that was all.

The police were quickly on the scene, and the body was immediately identified as that of David Thomas. He was conveyed to his own house. The younger Roberts, who with his father had been attracted to the spot, actually assisted in carrying him to the house - something that was greatly discussed afterwards.

On the night of the murder, Mrs Thomas dreamed that someone very dear to her had met with an accident, causing death. In her dream she saw men running away from the scene. The dream was so vivid that, rising early next morning because of her alarm at her husband's failure to return home, she spoke of it to her children, who were in bed. Within twenty minutes of this conversation, she learned that her husband had been killed within a stone's throw of the house. Mrs Thomas and her children were prostrate with grief and for some time she was out of her mind.

The police acted promptly and arrested John Thomas, Edward Roberts and his son as the last persons seen with the murdered man. It was proved however that John Thomas had left the deceased at the stile and gone to his own home. He was discharged from custody at the first magistrates' examination. Both Robertses denied their guilt, and Edward Roberts stated 'I know nothing at all about it. I never saw Mr Thomas last night at all'.

That remark was obviously untrue as there were many witnessess to the fact that all four men were drinking together at the *Duke* and that they left the inn together. The Robertses' cottage was searched and a blood-stained pocket handkerchief containing £66 in gold and a sovereign with a hole in it were found in a dark cupboard. The following morning the police discovered a billhook which bore traces of blood.

Two or three days after the men were taken into custody, a conversation between them was overheard by an officer who was in the corridor of the police station. Edward Roberts remarked, 'It is a bad thing their finding all that money upon him, and having none the night before'. Whereupon the elder prisoner observed, 'He can say that he was saving up for Christmas' and David Roberts said, 'Yes, I will tell them I was saving it up to buy a new suit of clothes or something of the sort'.

With the exception of this conversation, there was very little to establish the complicity of Edward Roberts in the crime and, in view of the son's complete exoneration of his father, it was thought to be very doubtful if any jury would convict. David Roberts was determined to clear his father of any involvement in the crime. David had always been wild and difficult and few could be found who had a good word for him. In 1877 he had enlisted in the Royal Scots, but of the seven years he served, five were spent in military prison, and he was finally discharged as 'incorrigible'. His only admirable trait was his dogged devotion to his father, and it was this no doubt that led to the following confession:

> On the night of 30 October 1885, I was in the house in which I live in Llanblethian between 7 and 8 o'clock. John Thomas, the deceased's nephew, came to me and asked if I would go to Cowbridge. I told him I did not like to go because it was so wet and windy. He told me if I could come with him I would not stand out in the wet. I knew then what he meant by that, he meant to stand a drink, and so he did, in Warren's public house [the *Bridge Inn,* in Eastgate, at the junction with the Limes. Solomon Warren was the tenant]. We had a "blue" [a nineteenth-century measure] each there, and then left to go home, but we came to the *Duke of Wellington* and I said, "Let's see if my father is in there". So we went in, and my father was in there, and David Thomas, Evans the Keeper, and

Lewis and Warren's son. I called for two blues of beer, which we put down to my father. Then we had a few games of cards for beer. Then we drew lots for more beer. We were in the *Duke of Wellington* until 11 o'clock.

David Thomas, his nephew, my father and I left the house together and it was a very wild night. We went with David Thomas as far as the Town Mill and there left him. David Thomas went over the stile by the pine end of the mill and we went to Llanblethian in a different direction. When we got to Llanblethian Mill John Thomas went in the direction of his house. I also wish to mention that my father, when he left the *Duke*, was what they commonly called "blind drunk" and I had to lead him home. I brought him home and put him to bed.

I am very sorry to say that after I had put my father to bed, I left the house by myself, took a big stick out of the house, and went to the top of Llanblethian Hill. I went down the footpath leading to Cowbridge and met the deceased coming up the footpath and asked him for his money. He asked me where I came from, and I said I came from Cowbridge. He replied, "Go to Cowbridge". I said, "I want your money first". I told him he had better give it to me or I'd make him. So we had a little struggle and I threw him down and struck him with the stick I had in my hand three times. Then I robbed him of all his money, and took all his papers which I burnt at home, the money bag also.

I also wish to state that when I did get home my father was in bed fast asleep. After I burnt everything I went to bed and got up next morning at 6.15 a.m. When I got up I went to the garden and counted the money because I did not want my father to know I had any money. He would want to know where I got it from, so I put the money where you found it, and nobody saw me put it there, my father being in bed at the time.

Also I wish to say that the weapon that I did the deed was the stick you had in court, not the billhook. I am the guilty person, and nobody else had anything to do with it. John Thomas and my father are innocent. David Roberts is my name. My life I now must part, for the murder of David Thomas.

Signed "David Roberts, son of Edward Roberts".

David's statement conveys the impression that he was seeking to minimise, as far as he could, the ferocity of the attack, and trying to give the impression that there had been no more than a slight argument between him and the victim which had unfortunately ended in blows. The 'little struggle' he alludes to was in fact a violent attack upon David Thomas that resulted in his being battered to death with three tremendous blows.

The confession does not ring true in other respects either. No stick could have produced such injuries as the dead man showed, whereas a billhook could certainly have inflicted them. Apart from the traces of blood on the billhook, it was wet, suggesting that it had been taken out by the murderer during the night. According to the confession, David and his father left David Thomas at the stile, not more than a quarter of a mile from his home. Even if the heavy wind and drenching rain and David Thomas's inebriated condition were taken into account, it should not have taken him more than ten minutes to get to his own doorstep. Yet, during this time, Roberts supposedly went home, assisted his father to undress, put him to bed, and then went out again to intercept his intended victim at a spot within 200 yards of his home. A huge question remains. Did David Roberts act alone?

Whatever the truth of the details of the confession, it would seem that Roberts was guilty. He was hanged in Cardiff prison on 2 March 1886.

SOURCES

Aberdare Times, 14 November 1885.
South Wales Daily News, 12 November 1885.
South Wales Echo, Special edition, 12 November 1885.
South Wales Police Museum, Police Headquarters, Bridgend.

SOME MEMORIES OF COWBRIDGE

By Selwyn Davies

[Councillor W. Selwyn Davies (1905-86) wrote the following reminiscences for the Cowbridge parish magazine in 1978. (This was about the time that the newsletter of the Cowbridge History Society was starting.) His articles are included in this book to commemorate the last mayor of the Borough before local government reorganisation in 1974; they evoke the character of the town as it was a hundred years ago. The author mentions his grandmother; she was Mrs Mary John, who lived for many years at Preswylfa, 30 Westgate. Ed.]

Some Memories of Cowbridge, 1914-1918

I was actually living in Cardiff when the 1914-18 War broke out, but came to Cowbridge for school holidays. One of the first things that I remember is that a volunteer corps was formed and trained on the cricket field under Mr Vivian Gwyn, a partner of Messrs. Gwyn and Gwyn, solicitors, and ex-Sergeant-Major Bill Brown, whose wife was for many years town hall caretaker. This force was eventually disbanded and the men had to enlist through official channels. Later on, enlisted troops trained in a field which is now the new market. This adjoined the bottom wall of my grandmother's garden, and I remember remonstrating violently with the sergeant-major for shouting and swearing at the soldiers.

I came to live here in 1916. Rationing came, and I believe the Food Office was where the dry cleaners is now [35 High Street]. A depot was opened at Pickard's shop (where the Rural District Council offices used to be, in Eastgate) for the reception of comforts for the troops, organised voluntarily by the ladies of the town.

The north side of the Stalling Down was ploughed up for potatoes, and the Welsh Allotment Association cultivated it. Incidentally, the memorial on the south side is to the men of the Glamorgan Yeomanry who trained there.

If I remember rightly, unlike during the War of 1939-45, there was no blackout in force, and the services at the Church and chapels continued normally. The Rev. Isaiah Roberts was the vicar, followed by the Rev. L. Hopkin-James.

Every now and then there would be entertainments at the Town Hall when gifts were presented to soldiers home on leave.

At the Grammar School, the staff were depleted, and consisted of the headmaster, the Rev. W. F. Evans, a master unfit for military service, the curate, the Rev. D. N. Davies, who was part-time, and Mr J. P. Marks, the organist. I only recall one lady teacher, Miss Davies from Eglwysbrewis, who taught music.

Ash Hall, Ystradowen, and New Beaupre were turned into hospitals for wounded soldiers. Those who could walk came into town in blue uniforms and were entertained to tea by the townspeople.

The master who was unfit formed a small orchestra from the Grammar School boys, and we used to go to Ash Hall and New Beaupre to play. Whether the patients improved or deteriorated after our efforts I cannot say!

Cowbridge was a big centre for the collection of hay for the feeding of the cavalry horses, and many a truck was transported from Cowbridge station to military depots. This was very unpopular with local farmers.

You will, of course, be aware of the very close connection earlier in the century between the Church and the Grammar School. A point of interest is this - during my years at the school (1917 to 1921), it was compulsory for the scholars (day boys and boarders, churchmen or nonconformists) to attend a short morning service on saints' days, for it meant we then had a half day! I do not know when this practice ceased.

I think the first lady driver in the town was my second cousin, Mrs Helen Miles, wife of E. W. Miles, solicitor, Taynton House [23 High Street], whose practice was taken in turn by Mr Wayne Morgan (father of Mrs Dr Evan Thomas), Mr Gaskell and now, of course, Mr Thornley Taylor.

I referred to rationing. I cannot remember the quantities of the various foods we were allowed, but I do remember that dripping was a valued substitute for butter or margarine. We picked nuts, blackberries, watercress etc, which made quite a contribution to the larder at various seasons.

For the first time, I think ladies appeared in banks as clerks, and there was, I believe, a lady postman.

We had Belgian refugees. I do not remember how many, but some lived in a house in Westgate where Mr and Mrs Davies live now.

One last thing, I think my only visit to the tower of Cowbridge Church was when the bells rang out on November 11th, 1918!

Some Further Memories

I think I had better start at Cardiff where I was born, and from where I came as a babe in arms and frequently during the years to Cowbridge. Leaving Cardiff on a stopping train, we ran through the delightful lower reaches of the Ely river, through Ely, St Fagans and Peterston-super-Ely to Llantrisant, where we changed from the G.W.R. to the Taff Vale Railway.

Llantrisant station had four platforms, including an island and a bay. There could be four trains there at once - Cardiff/Swansea; Llantrisant/Penygraig in the bay; and the Cowbridge train on the left-hand side of the island platform. Alas the station is no longer there, trains running non-stop from Cardiff to Bridgend. The Cowbridge train had come from Pontypridd, having crossed the main lines to get to the platform. The train usually consisted of two coaches, with an engine in the middle and controls at either end of the coaches. In effect, the engine propelled while the driver in control navigated the train. Five minutes to Llanharry station, which had a stationmaster and also a slip-off into a limekiln and another to the iron ore works.

Across Ystradowen Moors with a down gradient and a rollicking forty m.p.h. to Ystradowen station, again with a stationmaster (Bill Lewis whose son lives in Cowbridge) and a siding for the sawmills. Next, Maindy and Trerhingyll halt - a high-sounding name but just a plain wooden platform with a corrugated iron shack, as was Aberthin halt a mile on. Slow up for the staff to be passed to the signalman, and into Cowbridge station, and Stationmaster Williams, whose son Frank is a staunch churchman of ours. Now this is a comparatively new station, built for the extension of the level to Aberthaw. The old station was where Druids Green estate is now, and consisted of a covered platform, several sidings, an engine shed and goods offices. Two or three engines would be depoted here and a medley of trucks, carrying hay, fertilizers, agricultural machinery, livestock and, of course, coal. It was a hive of activity, and one of the outstanding characters there was Dan Punter, father of Gwilym. (I should have said that the journey from Cardiff, if there was a good connection at Llantrisant, took forty-five to fifty minutes.)

Cowbridge station had the honour of unloading and loading the King's bull, which was being exhibited at Cowbridge Show in the twenties and thirties.

Now if one wanted to get to the Leys or Barry, one caught one of the four or five through trains from Llantrisant, through a cutting, then Beaupre woods, first stop St Hilary halt, then St Mary Church Road station, Llanbethery halt and Flemingston Moors, St Athan Road station and eventually Aberthaw Low Level. In passing, I would say that the stations between Llantrisant and Cowbridge were in, or very adjacent to, the places whose names they bore, but the ones between Cowbridge and Aberthaw were quite a distance from the villages involved. At Aberthaw the train would be pushed into the sidings, while the engine went off back to St Athan Road to do some shunting with lime trucks. The passengers would proceed up a hill, under a bridge carrying the Bridgend to Barry line, and into Aberthaw High Level to entrain for Barry. Before the War, this line carried a very important train known as the Port to Ports Express. Starting at Swansea, then Port Talbot, Bridgend, through Llantwit, Aberthaw, Barry, Barry Docks and Penarth, it arrived at Cardiff whence it travelled over the G.W.R. to Banbury, the old Great Central to Sheffield, Great Northern to York, and the North Eastern to Newcastle, taking, I think, about ten hours. It was composed of G.W.R. coaches one day and Great Central the next, and had a restaurant car. There was a through coach to Hull.

There were, I think, about ten trains a day between Cowbridge and Llantrisant, the first leaving here about 7 a.m. and the last arriving here about 11 p.m., known as the Rodney, because if one was not a very respectable character one was known as a Rodney. Can anyone tell me why? The engines later on were usually 0-6-2 tank engines - for the uninitiated, this is translated as the front bogies, six couple driving wheels and two trailing wheels under the small tender or coal bunker. There were about five or six coaches. As there were no buses then, the trains were well patronised. They were happy, carefree and relaxed days, and I think we are far worse off by the passing of them. At least the trains did run, whereas these days the buses do not!

Alongside the road from Cowbridge station to Eastgate were allotments tilled mostly by railwaymen. The fire and ambulance stations are there now.

When Cowbridge became a station of some importance, houses were built for the employees in what is now known as Croft Street. It used to be called Taff Street.

A bus service to Cardiff and eventually to Bridgend was started by Mr Albert Maddox. Owing to the amalgamation of the railway companies, the Taff Vale Railway was taken over by the G.W.R. and the connections at Llantrisant became more harmonised. As a result the Cowbridge youth began to find jobs in Cardiff, for it was easier at this early stage to go by train as the early bus service was not so frequent. Then the South Wales Commercial Motors (which later became the Western Welsh Omnibus Company) took over Maddox's service, and at the outset there was an hourly service to Cardiff, Bridgend and Porthcawl, augmented later on by one from Cardiff to Neath.

FURTHER READING

Chapman, Colin, *The Cowbridge Railway* (Poole, 1984).
Richards, John, *The Cowbridge Story* (Bridgend, 1956). This book includes a photograph of Maddox's bus on p. 131.
Williams, Stewart, 'South Wales Commercial Motors', *Glamorgan Historian,* vol. 1 (1963), pp. 180-6.

INDEX